The Leopard Print Luggage

UZBEKISTAN

by

Richelle da Costa

ISBN:0987564935
ISBN-13:978-0987564931

2

CONTENTS

Author's Note:

The Leopard Print Luggage

I'm an adventurous woman, a cat lover, and a lioness at heart, so when leopard-print reappeared on the fashion scene, I couldn't help but embrace it.

It all began in Port Douglas, in Far North Queensland, where I was holidaying with a friend. We were indulging in a little retail therapy when I spotted a smart leopard-print handbag with a matching clip-on change purse. I just had to have it! Fifteen minutes later, I bumped into Jeanne two shops down, who insisted that I try on a slinky leopard-print slip dress and matching headscarf. Well, who would've thought!

Six months later, and with a bit more help from my friends, my faux fur collection had grown considerably and now included singlet tops, jackets, tights, underwear, scarves, hair clips, earrings, candles and ridiculous shoes with leopard-print bows. But on Christmas Day, when I unwrapped The Leopard Print Luggage, I knew there was no turning back. It was time for a real adventure, time to unleash those repressed feline instincts in the wild!

The luggage—smart, stylish, compact, robust and versatile—was designed for just the sort of travel experiences a leopard-print girl craves, experiences that will take her out of her comfort zone and offer new lessons and challenges. She must be willing to take risks…

My first journey through Turkey, northern Greece, Albania, Croatia, Slovenia, Italy and Romania, proved to be a great adventure, igniting an insatiable wanderlust and spawning the *Leopard Print Luggage* travel narrative series.

More journeys followed, and more stories:

Three Summers in Portugal, an intensely personal, romantic story spanning three years and three consecutive journeys to Portugal, with historical, geographical and cultural aspects woven into the narrative;

Armenia, an impetuous tour of discovery through this enigmatic, pocket-size Christian nation with my then-partner Tim, full of the sort of surprises and challenges which are guaranteed to make or break a relationship;

And now… *Uzbekistan.*

Chapter 1

Tashkent

Tashkent, at midnight, is a myriad of sparkling stars beneath an inky black sky.

The plane slides onto the runway, turns, then taxies towards the terminal. I'm feeling very excited at the prospect of once again being in an Oriental culture; the Moorish touches to the airport suggest that Uzbekistan is a country which will carry its Islamic traditions with it into a western-dominated future.

My fellow passengers are jostling to retrieve their belongings from overhead lockers. Most of them are quite ordinary-looking people—average, middle-class, white Caucasian tourists on their annual two week holiday, most likely. I had imagined a less conventional, fringy group.

We had boarded this flight in Riga. Seated in the second row, I found myself surrounded by members of a Swedish tour group who were intent on sitting together, even though their allocated seats were scattered. I had obliged by agreeing to swap, and as a result ended up beside Christina, an ex-diplomat with a wonderfully wicked sense of humour. It was her first-ever flight with a budget airline and she was finding it a somewhat illuminating experience.

Some in her group had paid for a meal; it soon became obvious that she wasn't one of them. We agreed that this could be a good thing—the pre-packaged dinners in their tacky cardboard boxes looked far from appetising. We decided to splurge on gin and tonics and brave the á-la-carte menu. I chose a chicken salad which, with my left-over marinated olives and baguette from Paris, was quite palatable. Christina's coarse rye sandwich went untouched—she was too busy anyway, familiarising herself with the peculiarities of 'cattle-class' amenities.

She returned from a visit to the washrooms, incredulous that on the entire plane there were only four. 'Business class has to line up with the rest of us,' she joked and had us both cackling hysterically about the 'caves', the makeshift sleeping tents for the hostesses and stewards, which had been set up across the last three rows of seats. She'd *never* seen this before, it would never be *allowed*, she ruminated, and insisted that she had seen a male and female emerging from same cave.

'Is this *The Baltic Way?*' she asked, in her heavily accented English.

In her intelligent company the flight passed quickly.

◆◆◆

The cabin doors open now, precipitating a frenzied rush

towards the forward and rear exits. Christina and I sit back and wait until the congestion clears, then make our way down the back stairs and across the tarmac, joining the queue in the busy arrivals lounge. Christina's tour leader assembles her group and they are whisked through customs, while I am left standing, somewhat bewildered, scanning the area for a visa office.

I find it way over on the left and make my way there, weaving through the crowd, pulling the Leopard Print Luggage along behind me. The imperious leader of another large tour group, a Russian I believe, pushes ahead of me at the window, clutching a wad of two dozen or so passports. He motions for me to fall in behind... Very generous, I *don't* think.

I'm hoping my scanned 'Letter of Introduction to Uzbekistan' will not present the same challenge as it had earlier that day at Charles de Gaulle Airport—Air Baltic had expected the original document, rather than the copy which had been emailed to me only two days before by the feckless tour company in Australia.

As I wait, I see a young boy on the other side of the barricade waving a sign bearing my name in large black letters. 'Ms Costa, Ms Costa!' he calls out, scanning the crowd. I wave to him and point to the visa window. I had booked a hotel transfer, so I relax now, reassured that people know I am here.

Ten minutes later, when it's my turn at the window, I pass my letter to the official. Clicking his tongue and shaking

8

his head, he consults the computer screen.

'One hundred US Dollars,' he barks. My tour agent had quoted somewhere between $65 and $85, so I pass him $85.

'This is all I have,' I state firmly.

'Wait,' he says. 'You will leave Uzbekistan on May 26?'

I nod.

'Then it will be eighty-five.'

'Mm,' I respond, wishing I had started lower.

He leafs through my passport, *oohing* and *aahing* at the various stamps. Then, stopping at a blank page, he glues in the Uzbek visa. Yes, it certainly *is* the most attractive of all.

I am pleased to see that the boy with the sign is still waiting; he has resorted to helping other passengers fill out their custom declaration forms. He introduces himself as Dadaxon; I assume that he is the tour guide. He presents another young boy, who takes charge of my documentation, all in Arabic script. He indicates that I must declare the amount of cash that I have brought in and seems surprised that I have only twenty-five Australian dollars plus a few odd euro coins. I show him my itinerary and he copies down the name of the tour company and the hotels.

Dadaxon then escorts me through customs and hands me over to a taxi driver, Ibi, who at least looks old enough to drive. He opens the boot, but when I signal that I want The

Luggage inside with me, he bows courteously and places it on the seat beside me. So far, so good!

Ibi babbles on as we speed into the city. Even though I can't understand a word of what he is saying, I appreciate his efforts to be friendly.

At 2 a.m. the wide, dark boulevards are understandably deserted. Many of the larger buildings and public places are flood-lit; again I notice that aesthetically pleasing blend of European and Islamic architecture.

We make a left-hand turn, mount a ramp, and arrive at the entrance of the Shodlik Palace Hotel. (My agent had nicknamed it the 'Shoddy Palace', but I assure you, there is nothing downtrodden or second-rate about this place.) Despite the hour, the receptionists in the foyer are cheerful and welcoming.

'We speak English,' they assure me, as they recite by rote: 'Welcome, we hope you had a pleasant flight, here is your key.' My enquiries relating to cash vending machines and rendezvous' with tour guides are met with blank looks—all of that will have to wait.

My room on the seventh floor looks impressive, but I'm too exhausted to take it all in. After a quick shower I fall onto the luxuriously-soft bed. Tomorrow I must learn the Uzbek word for *thank you*.

✦✦✦

'Rahmat,' I say confidently to the waitress six hours later in the grand brocade-and-chiffon dining room, as she delivers a good strong cup of tea. No response—perhaps I got the pronunciation wrong. I try again, rolling the *r* and nasalising the *h*. She flashes me a winning smile and steers me towards the 'Shodlik Open *Buffer* Breakfast,' artfully arranged on a circular benchtop in the centre of the room.

I'm not sure where to begin. To my left are bowls of smooth black raisins, plump dried apricots, tiny unhulled peanuts, three varieties of porridge, jugs of runny yoghurt and milk, and pitchers of thick apple juice. Then there are pancakes, rolled and filled with soft cheese and rice, and wedges of what looks like a vegetable frittata. Further on are trays of sliced meats, cheeses, bread and fruit. A veritable feast, and not a hint of *buffer* in sight! I fill my plate, eat what I can, then wrap the left-over caraway bread and cheese in a napkin for later, just in case.

Back out in the lobby, I notice that the currency exchange office is open. Two young girls are sitting behind the glass window, looking poised and efficient. I pass them my travel card, but they shake their heads, pointing to a small black machine.

'No cards,' one says. (I'm not sure if this means the machine is broken, or that they only deal in cash.)

I ask again at the reception desk, but get the same negative response.

'Map of Tashkent?' I ask next.

'No.'

'240-volt adapter?' (I have left mine in the hotel room in Paris). I draw a picture.

'Wait...' The receptionist climbs onto a chair and rummages in an upper cupboard. 'No,' she announces. 'Sorry.'

I shrug enquiringly, holding up my picture and pointing this way and that.

'Supermarket this way,' she indicates. 'Do you want taxi?' she adds.

'No money!' I reply, suppressing a laugh. The joke is lost in translation, but we do manage to reach an agreement that I can charge food and drinks to my room account until my tour leader arrives.

So, I have a day in.

I unpack, read, go down to the bar for coffee, send some emails, go back to the bar to buy a bottle of wine, take it back to the room and eat a lunch of breakfast left-overs and the last of my Parisian olives. I sing some scales, do a few Sudoku puzzles, update my journal, have a short nap, then return to the foyer, hoping to connect with some fellow tour group members.

There's no-one there, so I look in the bar. As on my previous two visits, it's empty. I decide to try the local vodka. 'How much?' I ask the bar-boy.

'Four thousand *sum*,' he responds. Cutting off the noughts and dividing by two, I calculate that this should equate roughly to two Australian dollars.

I nod, 'Yes, please,' and watch while he pours a generous slurp into the glass. It's chilled, and good.

Taking a table by the window, I am surprised to see that the sun has set; the trees in the leafy courtyard are no more than dark shadows. Accustomed to the long, light evenings in Paris, darkness at seven o'clock seems strange. Then, in the corner, I notice a man with a look about him that suggests he may speak English. He's drinking beer and gets up to order another.

After exchanging *hellos*, we are soon chatting away. His name is Grant, he works for a Canadian tour company and during his break, he is researching a possible 'adventure' package, which will take in Turkmenistan, Kazakhstan, and Tajikistan; like me, he finds this part of the world fascinating. He asks about my itinerary here, and just as I begin to tell him, his phone rings. 'A local contact,' he whispers. 'Must fly. Flick me an email,' he adds, passing me his card as he rushes off.

The vodka slides down and I realise I'm hungry. In the restaurant, most of the tables are occupied by a German group, enjoying their evening meal and noisily recapping the highlights of their day. I recognise a few faces from breakfast and we exchange friendly greetings.

I order pizza and pour some wine from the bottle I've

brought down from the room. (I tell myself it's really not that bad, but it must be—I only have one glass.) I've also brought a book to read but I can't seem to get past the first page. The pizza take ages and by the time it arrives I've lost my appetite.

I return to my room, suspended in that strange jetlagged state, somewhere between exhaustion and hysteria. I go to bed, but I can't sleep. My head is aching, full of pessimistic thoughts and bizarre images, fuelled most likely by the vodka.

People had warned me about Uzbekistan. 'It's dangerous,' they insisted, but I wouldn't listen. Then, just before my departure, I had a strange dream, featuring the word *TRIARJE,* in vivid capital letters. Worried that it might somehow be related to the ominous crisis-care *triage*, I had spent ages researching the dream word, but apart from an obscure reference to centurions and foot-soldiers in a language called Bosnian-Latin, I could find nothing.

I take a panadol and start to count backwards from twenty-nine, breathing deeply…

᠊᠊᠊

The bed is shaking. I open my eyes, tracking the origin of a strange clacking sound. It's the coat-hangers, rattling against the side of the wardrobe.

'Great! An earthquake,' I mutter, sitting bolt upright, remembering my dream. (Perhaps it was *triage* after all. I had imagined some horrific terrorist attack or bloody revolution, with me prioritising mangled victims according to their relative proximities to death. I hadn't even *thought* of a natural disaster.)

The shaking continues for at least a minute, the whole building creaking and groaning. Then it stops. I don't panic, but I do compile a mental list of the essential items I will grab in the event of the hotel collapsing—passport, phone, computer, camera, glasses, my favourite necklace from Lagos. And no more sleeping naked. Reaching down for the leopard print slip-dress on the floor, I pull it on. I even consider checking the location of the escape stairway (in disaster movies they never use the elevators), but I resist.

❦❦❦

I must eventually have gone back to sleep, because when I next check my watch it's half past nine. I wonder whether the quake may have been a dream, but for the moment there are more pressing priorities to deal with—I have no money, and the 'Buffer Breakfast' will finish in thirty minutes.

In the dining room, people are behaving quite normally; all seems to be in order. I approach a Russian-looking girl, moving about with a certain air of authority.

15

'Last night... ' I begin, shaking my whole body up and down.

'Ah,' she responds. 'Don't worry—just a small one.'

Feeling vaguely reassured, I scrutinize the other diners, looking for prospective tour group members. None so far fit my criteria.

Just then a bearded gentleman enters, in his sixties probably, alone. A minute later he is joined by a small, grey-haired woman, his wife I presume. The man gets up, goes to the buffet table and pours himself a glass of fruit juice. I decide to introduce myself. His name is Mark, he is a New Zealander and yes, he and his wife, Rae, are booked on the tour. They too felt the earthquake in the night, and they too were assured by the hostess that there was nothing to worry about.

Over breakfast, we exchange arrival stories. They had flown in early the previous morning on an airbus from China, and joined a long queue in the congested terminal. Obtaining their documents had been a nightmare of misunderstandings and frustrations, culminating in Mark losing the customs declaration form necessary for his return departure. Comparatively, my entry had been a breeze. However, they had only paid $65 for their visas.

We speculate about the size of our group. Rae and Mark are of the opinion that we will be just three—my name (and only mine) appears with theirs on their Letter of Introduction.

They are also under the impression that the formalities of the tour won't begin until that evening. Rae, sweet and bird-like, produces a tour itinerary with pages of 'essential notes', which no-one had thought of sending to me. They have two copies, so she generously offers me one.

I turn immediately to the section on money. The notes recommend bringing in American dollars, and according to Mark and Rae's experiences so far, they are paramount, either as direct payment for various services, or for converting to Uzbek *sum*. The black market, Mark suspects, is rife, with taxi drivers and touts giving better exchange rates than the banks and hotels.

'Did you bring dollars?' he asks.

'Enough for the visa, but apart from that, no,' I reply bleakly.

The notes also state that there are no ATM machines in Uzbekistan. Oh dear! But Mark and Rae have found one in the Hotel Dedeman, a few kilometres away. They assure me that it is perfectly safe to walk there, so I set off immediately.

As per Rae and Mark's directions, I follow the main boulevard, Navoi Avenue, past palatial buildings set in immaculate gardens, tended by teams of women wielding scythes, rakes and millet brooms. Other women dressed similarly in bright floral house frocks, headscarves and fluoro jackets are patrolling the eight-lane highway, dodging cars to sweep gravel and rubbish into small piles in the gutters. There are uniformed soldiers everywhere.

The Dedeman is still nowhere in sight. Thinking I must be lost, I approach a mansion that *could* be a hotel and stand peering into a tinted window, unable to find a door. Just as I am about to move off, a man emerges and we begin a charade-like conversation. My attempts to portray an ATM machine result in him directing me to the parking station, but then he gets it... 'Bank-o-Mat!' he exclaims triumphantly, patting me on the back and congratulating himself on his cleverness.

'Bank-o-Mat here?' I ask, pointing to his building.

'No!' he replies, walking off and shaking his head incredulously.

I keep walking. A few blocks further on, I see a tall building topped with a giant decorative *Ð*. This has to be it. Armed guards stare me down as I stride confidently towards the revolving door; fortunately they stand aside and let me pass. Taking the stairs to the left of the lobby, I continue along the corridor as Mark had instructed and there it is, a big shiny bank-o-mat in the wall. I can't recall ever having been so pleased to see one before.

I slide in my card. The screen gives me an option in English, which is reassuring. Following the prompts, I withdraw the maximum amount, one hundred. For some crazy reason, I expect to get Uzbek sum (UZS), but no, I get American dollars instead, two fifty-dollar notes. So... I take them to the currency exchange window a little further down the corridor.

Again, behind the glass, sit two coiffed, efficient-looking girls. The blonde one stands, takes the dollars, turns to the safe behind her, extracts a wad of notes and places it in a money-counting machine. The second dark-haired girl tears two leaves from a printed pad and records the amounts presented and dispensed on both sheets, and states in clear, concise English, 'You must spend this sum.' I nod my agreement (that is certainly my intention) and sign both copies. She stamps each copy three times, gives me one, then duplicates the other, placing a piece of carbon paper between it and another blank sheet before feeding them both into some kind of printing device. A few clicks later, she presents me with a pile of 1,000UZS notes, one hundred and eighty-eight in all.

My next dilemma is how to transport this brick of money, discreetly, back to the hotel. I find a rest room and, locking myself in a booth, fill my money belt to brimming, and then stuff the remaining notes down the front of my dress. Draping my scarf so the ends disguise my significantly enhanced (if somewhat angular) bustline, I sweep down the corridor and through the foyer, pass nonchalantly beneath the security scanner, then climb the steps to the footpath. I walk briskly at first, but a kilometre or so on, when I realise that no-one is taking any notice of me, I relax, enjoying the warm sunshine and the streetscape.

I notice a woman emerging from a grandiose building signed in Arabic, carrying a few bulging plastic bags. This must be the supermarket the receptionist had referred to earlier. Curious, I venture inside and browse up and down the pristine, almost-deserted aisles; there seems to be more staff than customers. Everything is here (well, everything but alcohol, of course. It is a Muslim country, after all)— aisle after aisle of tinned and packaged goods, fresh and frozen meats, poultry, seafood, fruit and vegetables, cheeses, sausages, olives and bread, even electrical goods. A pretty young woman dressed immaculately in a striped uniform and clicking high-heels shows me a selection of adapters including a multi-national one, which I buy for the equivalent of a tiny one dollar fifty.

Now, for coffee.

Up ahead, I can see tables set out on the footpath, with patrons eating and drinking in the shade of bright umbrellas. The kitchen is, for some reason, set below street level. Leaning down at the window, I ask for *kofe*.

Looking up, a young man responds, 'Nescafé?' It will have to do, I'm desperate. From a stand on his right, he unclips a sachet of instant coffee and hands it up to me.

'Water?' I enquire, pretending to sip from an imaginary cup.

'No,' he replies.

Perplexed, I politely return the sachet and try the next window, another café. Aha, they have a menu on the wall *and* they have coffee—there is a picture of it, in a cup! 1800UZS the sign says. Ninety cents. Pretty reasonable really.

I take a seat at the cleanest-looking table, wriggling to adjust my *sum* padding, and soon my coffee is delivered. It's sweetened, possibly with condensed milk, but it *is* coffee, and it's palatable. I pay the boy two 1000UZS notes, but he returns one and gives me change as well. That transaction remains a mystery.

Back at the hotel, Rae and Mark greet me warmly in the foyer. They have just returned from the airport, where they discovered that Mark's lost customs declaration form was not so essential after all. 'Don't worry, we look after our tourists,' they were told. Despite the inconvenience, they are pleased all the same, to have an authorised replacement, just in case.

They are off to eat lunch, but I decide to stay in and perhaps get some sleep.

Mid-afternoon, my phone rings. It's the hotel receptionist, informing me that someone named Monika has arrived and she will be joining our tour. So, now we are four. Two minutes later, the phone rings again. 'This is Yusuf, your guide,' a heavily-accented voice announces. The hotel staff have directed him to me also, it seems. He will meet us in the lobby at six.

⬥⬥⬥

When I emerge from the lift a few minutes before the

appointed time, Monika is already there. Australians are distinctive, I reflect, even before they speak. But when Monika does speak, it's in a broad New Zealand accent. She explains that she has lived in Adelaide for most of her adult life, but was born in Wellington.

Mark and Rae arrive, followed shortly after, by Yusuf. He is friendly and confident, but a little vague about details. He consults a list and reads out the names of two other group members, Lawrence and Marion (not names I would normally associate with 'adventure travel'), who will not arrive until the following evening.

He then us gives a general overview of the tour and an agenda for tomorrow's activities. Rae raises the issue of the local payment of €200 which the notes say should be given to the guide at the commencement of the tour. Yusuf says he knows nothing about such a payment. Ok, we're fine with that. Even if we pay-as-we-go, we reckon we'll be way ahead.

We ask Yusuf to explain the protocols surrounding the local currency. He warns us not to deal with taxi drivers or touts, as unauthorised exchanges are illegal; he suggests rather, that we change money through *him*. Now we're more confused than ever, but his rates are as good as the taxi drivers' and his black computer bag always seem to magically produce whatever notes we require.

'The National Bank of Yusuf is open twenty-four hours a day,' he jokes.

Rae, Mark, Monika and I agree to go out for a meal together, a sort of 'get-to-know-you' occasion. Yusuf recommends a restaurant close by with a special Uzbek meal for just 80,000UZS (about $40) per person. We decline simultaneously and walk instead to a cool and pleasant outdoor eatery on the main street beside the canal, where tables are set up around a central garden. We order grilled lamb kebabs and *samsa*, golden pastry balls stuffed with tomato and spiced meat. Mark and Monikas' beers are tankard-sized; Rae and I ask for vodka and it arrives in a jug. The food is delicious and our waiter, whom we nickname Manuel (from *Fawlty Towers*), is delightful, darting here and there, creating a string of disasters.

During the meal, we share some basic information about ourselves. (Tour groups are strange sub-cultures. We spend a short time with complete strangers, divulging our life stories or perhaps inventing them, and then go our separate ways, usually never to meet again.) Rae and Mark, married, have recently retired, having sold their garden nursery business to one of their four daughters. They are ardent travellers and enjoy an adventure. Monika is a Doctor of Marine Biology, married to another Marine Biologist, with a young son, Chad. She has added Uzbekistan on to the back of a conference in Scotland. My own story—ex-teacher, ex-truant officer, ex-wife, now nomadic writer-musician with two daughters, two natural grandchildren and an ever-increasing number of de-facto ones—feels like a stark contrast. But, despite our diverse backgrounds, we seem pleased with each other.

Just as we are finishing our complimentary green tea, a group of women on the other side of the room get up from their table and begin to dance to the lively Uzbek music playing in the background. They step and weave, arms raised, using a repertoire of expressive hand movements, traditional gestures we assume. It's a joyful and unexpected finale.

Manuel brings the bill, a grand total of 32,000UZS—yes, about $4 each.

❀❀❀

Next morning at nine, Yusuf meets us in the foyer.

'We will go walking,' he announces.

It's bright and warm and we stroll off down the street, chatting away companionably.

At Navoi Avenue (named after Navoi, the acclaimed Uzbek poet), we turn to the left and follow the broad boulevard away from the city centre, with Yusuf pointing out various buildings and landmarks, mostly from the Soviet era. New Tashkent, he explains, with its avenues and gardens and monuments, is largely the legacy of the 1966 earthquake, which destroyed most of old city. Mark, Rae and I raise our eyebrows; Sabrina's comment about Monday night's 'small one' is suddenly making more sense.

'Here we will connect with the Tashkent Metro, the only one in Central Asia,' Yusuf says proudly, directing us down a marble stairway into an underpass. 'The design is very complex due to the unusual geological conditions.'

Indeed.

'There are twenty-nine stations and they are all works of art,' Yusuf goes on. 'Materials like metal, glass, plastic, stone and ceramics have been chosen for their strength and stability, but also for their beauty.'

This station, Alisher Navoi, is like a gallery, featuring depictions of characters from his works. 'More stations are planned, but there is a problem with the underground water,' Yusuf says, pointing to some suspiciously damp areas on the tunnel walls.

A sleek carriage emerges from the tunnel and we climb aboard, a little nervously. We pass G'ofur G'ulom station, (named after another Uzbek literary figure) and arrive at Chorsu, our destination, in the heart of the Tashkent's 'Old Town'. Emerging from the underground, we are immediately caught up in the vibrant throng of people heading towards, or returning from, Eski Zhuva bazaar.

Eski Zhuva has a rich history. Located at the junction of four ancient trade routes, it was, for centuries, the hub of the old city—a mecca for international trade but also the place where people congregated to hear news and rumours, to watch cock-fights, performing clowns and executions, and to listen to *hafize* singers and *maddahi* preachers. The caravanserais and craftsmen's quarters were here too, as was the Kukeldash Madrasah, the historic 16th century mosque and Islamic teaching school which still stands beside the Juma Mosque, on a small hill behind the bazaar.

Yusuf suggests we go there first.

The structure of Kukeldash, he explains, is standard for a madrasah, with two minarets flanking the main portal, and a double-storied square of rooms surrounding a central courtyard. The entrance, a vast archway, is decorated in striking turquoise and blue mosaic tiles. Passing beneath it, we are immediately struck by the beauty, quietness and palpable sense of reverence within.

The director of the school comes out to welcome us, proudly outlining the building's history and function. 'It has survived two earthquakes and served as a fortress and a hotel,' he says, 'but now, once again, it fulfils its original spiritual function as a *madrasah.*'

'A madrasah is an Islamic school,' he explains. 'This one offers two courses of study—a *hifz* course teaching memorization of the Qur'an and an *ālim* course which qualifies the candidate to be accepted as a scholar in the community.'

I ask if females can be enrolled. 'Yes, this is possible,' he says, 'but they will study separately from the men.'

'Now, please feel free to wander.'

We leave our shoes at the entrance, and move off in

different directions.

I venture first to the left, where a low doorway opens into a tiny, dimly-lit mosque. It's refreshingly cool inside. My feet encounter luxurious carpet and the bare, whitewashed walls seem to glow in the half-light. I linger as long as I dare, then return to the vaulted corridor leading to the green courtyard, shaded with plane trees. Following the mosaic brick pathway around the perimeter, I pass the ground-floor schoolrooms; a collection of shoes at the door signals that a class is currently in progress. Occasionally the curious face of a young boy appears, peeking out through an arched pane. Above, some older boys are hanging over the balcony, observing us.

Feeling like an intruder, I return to the portico, where the others are re-assembling. We leave a humble donation and continue on.

Back on the busy thoroughfare, we stop to take some refreshment in one of the many outdoor cafés. The caffeine-addicts (me included) decide to risk the coffee. It arrives in gaudy Disneyland mugs, sugary and bitter. All around us, groups of women, dressed in long coats and colourful headscarves are having morning tea together, surrounded by a ring of shopping bags and baskets.

Revived, we re-join the crowd surging towards the bazaar. Yusuf and the men stride on ahead; we girls stop to peer into shop windows and photograph black-eyed children selling cherries, walnuts and dried sunflower seeds in paper cornets.

27

A wide staircase leads up into the main body of the produce hall, a labyrinth of market stalls beneath a canopy of blue-tiled domes. The aisles are crowded and noisy with vendors calling out their prices and holding out handfuls of their produce as people pass. On Yusuf's advice, we sample any food which draws our attention, otherwise we could seriously insult the seller. Sunny Uzbekistan abounds in sweet and juicy grapes, melons, apricots, pears, apples, quinces, peaches, pomegranates, figs and berries, and they are all here. We move along the rows, biting into ripe-red raspberries and cubes of pink watermelon, and dipping our fingers into fragrant cones of turmeric, cumin, coriander and fennel. Plastic buckets overflow with star anise, nutmeg kernels and over-sized cinnamon sticks, and sachets of saffron threads, priced like gold at home, go for a few thousand *sum*. Butchers wheel trolleys laden with great slabs of meat ready to be carved up on demand, young girls push babies' prams stacked with rounds of hot Tashkent bread, and loud music blares out through loudspeakers.

In the vegetable hall, plump cheerful women are spraying salad leaves with glistening water droplets and arranging radishes, tomatoes and bell-peppers on benches beside aubergines, cucumbers, okra, beets, cabbages and carrots. Potted herbs stand in rows on the dusty floor beside bulging sacks of pistachios, walnuts, almonds and peanuts, and solemn, vigilant children preside over jars of honey and molasses, and the family's preserved fruits and jams.

Monika calls me to join the rest of the group near a back

exit, where most of the stalls are devoted to rice, pulses and pastas of all shapes and sizes. Others, decorated with garlands of braided onions and garlic, sell exotic root spices—kumera, turmeric, ginger and horseradish. I stop beside a row of cardboard boxes piled with small, white balls. These are *kurt*, made from sour milk, Yusuf says, holding one up for me to sample. Quite unpleasant, I decide. Other boxes hold shards of transparent crystallised rock. Salt perhaps? I pick up a piece, instinctively running my tongue over its cool, chalky surface. 'For child-bearing,' Yusuf explains, grinning. We both laugh as I quickly wipe my mouth with the back of my hand and drop the piece back in the box.

Just outside there are eggs, thousands of them—tiny speckled quail eggs, brilliant-white over-sized duck eggs and middle-sized coffee-coloured hens' eggs. And in the car parks, farmers are loading bulging sacks of potatoes, carrots and parsnips directly from their trucks and trailers into car boots and wheel barrows.

The delicious smells of grilled kebab and spatchcock remind us it's time for lunch. Yusuf leads us away from the market and across the road to a busy side street lined with eating houses where he hopes we will be able to eat *plov*.

'Plov?' we ask, intrigued.

'Uzbekistan's national dish,' he explains. 'You will love it!'

But today we are too late for plov. It is served only in the middle of the day, he says, and to our surprise, it is already after two. We make do with more of the spicy lamb *shasliks*, served simply with a garnish of finely sliced white onions and freshly baked bread sprinkled with toasted cumin seeds.

❦❦❦

Back outside, Yusuf hails two unmarked taxis. They're private cars he says, which ferry passengers to and fro for a cheaper price. He negotiates a fee with both drivers and we depart, racing down the main thoroughfare and finally screeching to a halt outside an old mosque, where a team of men are working on wooden scaffolding way above, re-configuring the damaged mosaic panels above the entrance portal. On the ground below, the tiles are laid out in the order of the pattern, waiting to be winched up, segment by segment, to the work platform.

As we watch, another car pulls up. An old gentleman and two women alight, obviously in awe of this edifice. The man carries a cloth bag bulging with what we discover are walnuts; he places mounds of them in our open palms, blessing us. Yusuf explains that his visit to the mosque is a type of pilgrimage and he has brought the bounty of nuts from his farm outside the city as an offering.

The mosque is closed due to the renovations, so we walk on to Teleshayakh, another mosque complex close by. As we pass a huge mound of rubble, I notice among the lumps of smashed concrete, bright fragments of broken tile. No one seems to be looking, so I ferret around until I find a pretty blue and yellow piece, and quickly stow it in my handbag… a precious souvenir.

Teleshayakh is expansive, and laid out, like Kulkedash, in the traditional manner of a medrasah, but rather than housing school rooms, the cells surrounding the inner courtyard are occupied by master craftsmen. There are wood and metal workers, calligraphers, painters, embroiderers and jewellers, all producing exquisite objects, for sale of course. This is not really the place to bargain, Yusuf advises, as these items are of the best quality.

I am fascinated by the painted gourds with bright plaited chords for carrying or hanging. One of these, tureen-shaped and hand-painted in cobalt blue, gold and white, demands my attention. It seems very expensive, one hundred euros, and even though I appreciate the skill of the master (samples of his work are featured in the *Uzbekistan Air* flight magazine), I hesitate to finalise the purchase. I'm worried, most of all, about how I will carry the gourd from country to country without damaging it—it's feather-light, but, I suspect, fragile. He won't reduce his price, but offers to include the two small water scoops that he is working on right now. Yusuf assures me that this price is very reasonable for the quality. I leave a deposit of 10,000UZS and arrange to return in ten days to collect the completed set.

In another cell further along, the girls buy colourful silk scarves and cushion covers; I come away with a striking brass pendant, ornately-patterned in enamel and strung with leather.

I'm ready to go back to the hotel now, but today's program is far from over.

Yusuf hails another pair of taxis and we head off to Hazrati Imam, a religious centre, famous for its library which houses the *Ottoman Koran*, the most famous holy book of Islam in the world. Dating back to the 7th century, this Koran has travelled to Medina, Damascus, Bagdad, Samarkand, St Petersburg, Ufa, and finally to its resting place here, in a temperature-controlled glass casket beneath the dome of the Tilla-Sheikh mosque. We join the pilgrims standing in line—bearded men in dark suits and embroidered *tiubiteka* hats, and plump women in loose floral dresses and colourful headscarves, their faces alive with anticipation.

Soon it's my turn on the viewing platform. I'm surprised to find that the Koran is so much bigger than I expected—more than half a metre wide—and the calligraphy, inscribed onto thick, dark-grey deer hide, is stark and unadorned. It emanates a compelling energy, oozing history and intrigue.

The line of viewers shuffles along the platform, past the casket and down the stairs on the other side, to the library cells which contain a staggering 30,000 manuscripts and books from all over the Islamic world, including beautifully illuminated Korans in every language imaginable.

Back in our taxis once again, we disappear into the back

streets, bouncing along rough dirt tracks through modest courtyard communities. Craning our necks, we look for open doorways in the mud-brick walls, hoping for a glimpse of the gardens and tiny mosques hidden within.

Our next destination is the Museum of Applied Arts, once the handsome private home of a rich 19th century merchant. The main entrance hall, with its elaborately carved and painted walls, pillars and ceilings, is an attraction in itself. The other grand rooms display ceramics, jewellery, wood-carvings, musical instruments and textiles, such as coats, hats, rugs, and the gorgeous needlework cloths called *suzanis*. I try on a pair of embroidered ankle boots, similar to a pair I bought in Istanbul three years ago. Yusuf claims that they would certainly have been made in Uzbekistan. He could well be right.

Last on the agenda is Amir Temur, the city's oldest square, which is actually *round* like the sun, with eight streets running off it like rays to the outskirts of Tashkent. In the centre stands an imposing statue of the great military leader and statesman Tamerlane, who founded the powerful empire of the Temurids, reputedly spreading 'civilisation' and 'culture'. He is depicted here on horseback in warrior's attire, with one arm raised, apparently to signify reconciliation and concord. Historical accounts describe his campaigns as 'violent', 'aggressive' and 'relentless', but there is no doubt that they had a profound effect on world history, bringing together mathematicians, scientists, astronomers, architects and musicians.

Beneath Temur's statue, silhouetted now against a darkening sky, couples sit in quiet contemplation on benches set amidst colourful flowerbeds. We join them, sensing their reverence, as they survey the park and the stately buildings which surround it: the blue-domed Museum of the History of the Temurids, the grand baroque-style State Bank, the majestic buildings of the Tashkent State Judicial Institute, the Clock Tower erected in 1947 to celebrate the victory over fascist Germany, and Hotel Uzbekistan, the city's first 4-star, high-rise hotel.

It's 7 p.m. and we're worn out. We take the metro back to Navoi Avenue, eat a pizza-and-chai dinner in a street cafe, and return to the hotel, where we look about for our belated tour-mates, Marion and Lawrence. The foyer is empty, so we try the bar, which looks deserted as well. We decide to have a nightcap and discover in a dark corner, a sophisticated-looking couple, sitting side-by-side, tapping away on matching laptop computers. This could be them, we decide. Rae goes off to enquire (she's good at that sort of thing), but is instantly dismissed and returns a minute later, shaking her head.

We laugh about expectations. Rae and Mark divulge that they had first noticed me in the restaurant on the night of their arrival at the hotel. They had popped down for a cup of tea and had spotted me stuffing a bottle of wine into my handbag. They'd decided then and there that I was definitely a girl with 'spunk' and hoped I would be one of their group.

Yesterday, they confide, had been their 44th wedding

anniversary, all in all, a disaster. It had begun with the three frustrating hours getting through customs, followed by the loss of the customs form. The currency exchange office had been closed, so they'd been forced to change money with a rogue taxi driver, then on arrival at the hotel, they couldn't get the door to their room open (Mark was almost to the point of abusing the staff when they realised they were on the wrong floor). Finally, desperate for a drink, and perhaps an over-due celebration, they'd ordered whiskies in the bar, but later discovered that they'd been charged 80,000UZS (almost forty Australian dollars). They were still smarting about the whisky.

❦❦❦

Chapter 2

Samarkand

Lawrence and Marion *had* arrived the previous evening, but must have just missed us in the bar.

When we meet them in the dining room at breakfast time, we're pleased that they bear absolutely no resemblance to last night's computer snobs. Larry and Maz are, in fact, fresh from China, having spent the last two weeks roughing it in the foothills of the Qingling Mountains, tending endangered (and apparently cantankerous) pandas. Maz, a psychiatrist and her husband Larry, a psych nurse, live and work in Wangaratta, a town in northern Victoria. So, two more for the Aussie team. We don't have a lot of time to chat, as we must hurry to catch the 8.30 a.m. express train to Samarkand.

We take taxis to Tashkent station. By the entrance, officials are checking bags and documents, while businessmen pace impatiently and country folk push through, lugging crates of fruit and vegetables and live chickens. Inside, it's even more chaotic: the platforms are a seething mass of arriving and departing passengers; hawkers with street trolleys peddle steaming cobs of blackened corn, *pide* and ice-cold drinks; announcements blare out through loudspeakers; and attendants run about waving flags, shouting and blowing whistles.

We follow Yusuf to the fourth carriage of a waiting train and climb aboard. Then, in a confusing manoeuvre, he leads us across the corridor and out again onto the adjacent platform, where the beautiful blue SHARQ is waiting. Smart, uniformed attendants check our tickets and direct us to our reserved seats in one of the streamlined carriages decorated with white insignia, and soon we are off, leaving cosmopolitan Tashkent behind.

I gaze out the window, trying to shut out the jarring noise from the TV overhead, blasting out coarse Uzbek movies as we speed through the rural landscape. Pale, treeless fields of soft greens and milky browns flash by, dotted with bent-over figures—men in dark trousers and women in long skirts and headscarves—working side-by-side tending the sun-bleached crops. Villages are few and far between.

After an hour or so, attendants deliver tea and coffee in smudgy glass cups, full to brimming. Hot liquid sloshes everywhere as the train rocks and tilts. Hawkers follow, moving through the carriages offering meat pastries and sweets. One of them, a peasant woman, is peddling more of those sour-milk balls, lewdly, we suspect, judging from the joking and guffawing that surrounds the transactions.

The farming belt, meanwhile, has morphed into pastureland. Here and there, we see herds of grazing animals—black-and-white cattle, brown woolly goats, horses, donkeys and occasionally sheep—and every now and then, a mud-brick compound of crude, flat-roofed houses set around stockyards and animal shelters.

A surprising line of snow-capped mountains materialises, rising out of the flat plain on the far left-hand side, while on the right, the landscape becomes ever more arid. Make-shift irrigation channels of open concrete piping dissect the barren fields, waiting for rain, and scraggy livestock scavenge or lie listlessly beside low, scrubby bushes. A ramshackle factory appears, surrounded by piles of broken vehicles and further on, a cluster of identical, single-storied, cream-coloured brick houses, perched like monopoly toys on the cream earth. Close by, a row of rail carriages lies stranded in an abandoned siding beside a forlorn cemetery enclosed by rusted metal fencing. Yusuf said the journey would take three-and-a-half hours. It's already midday and Samarkand is still a word on the map.

The desert stretches on.

More old train carriages flash by; these ones, painted in gaudy blues, reds and greens, have been converted to makeshift dwellings, with shade-cloth verandahs and piles of stones suggesting fences and gardens. A few minutes later we pass a small village, beside what *could* be an oil rig, but is more likely a water bore, as the rooftop terraces here are draped with green grapevines. Incongruent, gaily-striped umbrellas add to the air of optimism and the small children standing beside the track, eyes riveted on the train, are smiling.

The terrain does indeed become greener and more undulating; there is even a muddy stream, snaking its way along a broad riverbed between two hills. On a far slope, an advertisement for UZ-DAEWOO is configured in fragments of white rock.

The train stops in the next town, for five or ten minutes. The houses here are neat and prosperous-looking, made of red rammed earth with roofs tiled in terra-cotta. While we wait, two teenage girls hang over the back of our seat, watching as I upload some photos onto my lap-top, laughing and exclaiming, and asking questions in English when they can.

Our journey continues. Three-and-a-half hours stretches to five. Finally, we are there.

We vote, unanimously, to eat before checking into our hotel. Yusuf announces, excitedly, that there is a restaurant nearby that serves Samarkand plov. He rings ahead and when we arrive, a table is set up for us in the cool garden, crowded with other plov-eating patrons.

The meal begins with a chilled yoghurt-and-cucumber soup, thick with fresh dill. Then the plov arrives—four platters of yellow-tinged rice, mixed with carrot, onion and chick peas, and piled high with gelatinous chunks of lamb. As well there are salads of sweet cherry tomatoes, lemon-soaked onion, and fresh green herbs.

'Plov is certainly popular here,' Mark comments, spooning a generous portion onto his plate.

'Yes, of course,' Yusuf responds. 'It is the king of Uzbek cuisine.'

'And there are hundreds of variations,' he elaborates. 'Each

39

region has its own special ingredient. There is plov with quince, with Turkish peas, barberries, eggs, even pomegranates, but the basic ingredients are the same—meat, rice, onions, carrots and oil.'

'Special occasions, like weddings, are celebrated with a plov feast,' he goes on. 'Then the family will call in an *oshpaz* (a master plov-maker), and when he and his team go to the market, it's always a spectacle. Vendors rush to put their best products on display as they move from one seller to another, examining onions, carrots and grains of rice, touching, smelling and tasting. If an oshpaz buys at one place, it is the best advertisement the seller could wish for. He will have success in trading for some time afterwards.'

Yusuf draws breath as pots of green tea arrive.

'Drinking green tea after eating plov, is another tradition,' he explains. 'And a very sensible one,' he adds, grinning, 'since only a very healthy person can drink vodka after a good plov.'

These plov stories are never-ending.

Satisfied with this, our very first plov, we proceed to The Golden Globe, our hotel for the next three nights—not swank like the Shodlik, but authentic and charming, and in my opinion, preferable. Miram, a stout, enterprising sort of woman, ushers us in, assailing us with offers of postcards, suzanis and alcohol, which she can surely 'arrange' for us.

We suspect that The Globe was once a grand house, with

rooms typically arranged around a central courtyard garden. There is even a swimming pool which, unfortunately, is empty. 'For the summer…' Miram explains. It's a hot day, but still spring, so we are out of luck.

She distributes the keys to the rooms—two doubles and two singles. We take the external staircase to the first floor where my room, and those allocated to Rae, Mark, Larry and Maz, open off a common vestibule; Monika's is further along.

Mine, typically overdone with velvet and chiffon, is huge, with a double bed and a single bed, a small table and two chairs beneath the window, a wardrobe, and a dresser, all in dark-stained timber. There is a bar fridge (set to maximum but not cold), a large TV set (which doesn't seem to work), and an air-conditioner (without a remote). The bathroom looks brand new, with glossy white-tiled walls, a mirrored vanity unit with movie-star lights, shelves displaying bottles of nasty bulk hair products, a plastic hair brush and a shiny new hair dryer. Cute!

Mid-afternoon, the group reassembles. The couples are incredulous that I have ended up with the biggest room, and the only one with a double bed. This seems perfectly reasonable to me, I joke. Is it because I have paid for a single supplement, or is it not common practice for Uzbek couples to share a bed? We're not sure.

The others go off to explore but I need an afternoon in, and some solitude.

Fetching my journal and my novel, I return to the courtyard, where a cool breeze wafts by, tinged with the heady fragrance of hibiscus. As I settle in, appraising the colourful suzanis and ceramic platters mounted on the walls, Miram pounces on me with her pile of postcards and her bulging bag of handicrafts, which she proceeds to lay out in front of me.

'Vodka?' I enquire.

'Yes, of course,' she responds, stuffing the postcards back in the bag.

'How much?' I ask, suspecting she may be out to make a quick profit. I am prepared to pay up to 12,000UZS, so that's what I offer. She takes the money and calls to one of the boys watching the TV in the foyer. He takes off with a mate down the street.

Five minutes later, Miram reappears, beaming, with the vodka (quite a good Russian one as it turns out), a glass, and a dish of sugary sweets, which taste like hard fondant icing.

Time flies and the explorers return. As I had suspected, the sights within walking distance of the hotel are the same ones we will visit tomorrow. Miram brings 'Welcome Tea', another plate of sweets, and a dish of ripe, black cherries.

Two pretty young women join us in the courtyard. They speak a little English and seem keen to befriend us. Tatyana has a baby, which has just gone down to sleep, and the younger girl, Nila, is pleased to announce that she is pregnant. They are from Andijan, further to the east, and are on holiday here with their husbands. Nila shows us some holiday snaps—posed group photos taken outside some of the Samarkand sights. She proudly points out her husband, 'I *love* my husband,' she croons, holding her hand over her heart. (The husbands are nowhere to be seen. We suspect they may be having a night out on the town.)

Then to our surprise, Nila produces a bottle of beer. Mark opens it with his teeth—a New Zealand party trick, he says—which causes great hilarity. The girls are very interested in knowing all our ages. (It is apparently the first question asked of a stranger in Uzbekistan.) They call Mark, the oldest male, 'grandfather', and defer to him from then on. The baby sleeps on and Tatyana brings a packet of something cold and squishy, and small plates for us all. It's very sweet ice cream, with a meringue-like texture. The girls spoon it out, serving Mark first, of course, and taking great care with the offering. The receptionist joins us, and then her grandmother, the robust matriarch of the family, who announces that she is eighty-six years old with thirty-seven grandchildren and great-grandchildren. Grinning broadly, she reveals two sets of gleaming, gold-capped teeth.

Maz and I go off to buy bread, cheese and sprat paté from the corner shop (against the recommendation of Miram, who says the owners can't be trusted), then in our delightful Samarkand courtyard, we share a picnic with our new family. Afterwards we teach the girls how to play cards. Tatyana brings a tiubiteka skull cap for Mark and the matriarch brings another for Larry, not the oldest, but a male none-the-less.

It's fun. We retire to bed, feeling grateful for this joyful exchange with the locals.

I drift off to sleep, then, all of a sudden, I am aroused by loud knocking. I catch my breath in the darkness, listening intently while the knocking continues. Then, creeping out of bed, I stand with my ear to the door. There it is again, but definitely not at my door. Could it be someone trying to get in the external door, the one into the vestibule? I decide to ignore it, and get back into bed. The knocking goes on, then I hear the sound of a knob turning and a door closing. I try to relax, but now I hear other muffled noises, a raised male voice, some dull thumps, distressed weeping, groans of perhaps an aggressively sexual nature, then silence.

I can't help but worry. The fourth room opening onto this vestibule is occupied by Nila, the younger of the two girls who had shared our picnic (and the one who had produced the bottle of beer). My imagination creates a disturbing scenario of her husband returning late and angrily meting out punishment to his erring wife. I toss and turn, contemplating the fate of this innocent next-door girl.

❧❧❧

In the morning, Nila's door is closed and all is quiet in the vestibule. Outside on the balcony, I pause to look down over the sunny courtyard and the breakfast table. I'm the last one down it seems.

As we devour our hearty meal of fried eggs, cake, bread, salami, cheese and fruit, I question the others about the knocking and the disturbing noises in the night. No-one seems to have heard anything, apart from Monika, whose room is next to Tatyana's. She remembers hearing voices, but that's all.

Yusuf collects us from the foyer and we go walking, up our street and into University Boulevard, with its strip of green parkland running along the middle, enclosed with fancy wrought-iron fencing. The footpath is busy on this gorgeously-warm morning, with men in suits, skull caps and briefcases off to work, pairs of school children walking hand-in-hand (the little girls in dark pinafores with frilly white blouses), well-dressed teenagers jostling outside the college, and women with bulging shopping trolleys returning from the market. Many of the younger ones are wearing long, colourful dresses and round pillbox hats with spangles and fringes; even those who prefer western garb have added a 'bling' element with sparkling jewellery, sequins and pretty high-heeled shoes. Their femininity is refreshing. As in cosmopolitan Tashkent, no-one takes too much notice of the soldiers who seem to be patrolling everywhere. Rae warns me not to photograph them. Too late!

We reach a leafy roundabout, with a seated statue of the great Amir Temur in the middle. The way to the right, a grand avenue lined with clipped mulberry trees, leads to Gur-Emir, the Tomb of the Kings, our first destination. Mulberry trees, Yusuf says, have been planted everywhere in the city and are tended by council workers and harvested in their entirety for the silk industry. We stop to sample the juicy, white berries (a much more practical colour, we decide, than the purplish-red that we're used to).

Even from a distance, Gur-Emir is impressive. Its one-cupola construction was the precursor and model for the great Mughal tombs of Humayan in Delhi, and the Taj Mahal in Agra, both built by Temur's descendents. Though weathered, it is nonetheless resplendent, with its azure dome and tiled walls decorated with a stunning array of geometric patterns and epigraphic ornaments against a background of pale terracotta bricks.

The sarcophagi of the great Temurids—Amir, his sons and two grandsons—are interred here. Slabs of onyx, decorated with refined oil paintings, line the lower walls of the mausoleum, topped with a striking stalactite cornice; above, the tessellated walls and fluted ceilings of painted plaster shimmer and glow with gold. Temur's marking stone, covered with a solid block of dark green jade, stands in the middle. Yusuf translates its inscription, adopting his favourite, oratoric tone: 'Anyone who violates my stillness in this life or the next one, will be subjected to inevitable punishment and misery.'

He goes on to relate how, in 1740, Temur's stone was

46

broken in two when a rival warlord, Nadir Shah, attempted to carry it off to Persia. The theft apparently heralded a run of bad luck for the Shah, including the near death of his son. When the stone was returned to Samarkand, his son miraculously recovered. According to another legend, Soviet archaeologists invoked Temur's curse when they opened his crypt during World War I, resulting in the invasion of Russia by the Nazis; a third claims that when the skeleton of Amir Temur was later put on a plane by the repentant Soviets and flown over the Allied armies retreating into Russia, the troops rallied, turning the tides and precipitating the defeat of the Germans. (We're not sure whether Yusuf subscribes to these superstitions, but he certainly enjoys the story-telling.)

Back outside in the yard, he leads us down a set of stairs to an excavated cavern which has been converted into a gallery and shop, displaying Samarkand handicrafts and antiquities. Mammaduli, the proud proprietor, assembles us in one corner and gives us a brief, emotional outline of Samarkand's history.

'My city is one of the oldest in the world,' he boasts, 'as old as Babylon, Rome and Athens. Perfectly placed in the fertile Zarafshan Valley in the heart of Central Asia, it was destined to play a key role in the historical, political, economic and cultural life of the region.'

'Over the centuries, there have been times of glory and periods of upheaval and decay. The city was invaded again and again and fell to Alexander the Great, the Arab Khaliphat and Genghiz Khan, thus this catacomb of

47

underground escape routes,' he elaborates, pointing to dark tunnels leading off in all directions. 'It was the centre of trade along the Great Silk Road from China to Byzantium and under the rule of Amir Temur it became the capital of the powerful state of Sogd, the centre of his great empire.'

'He was the one who cared most about the beauty and strength of the city,' Mammaduli continues. 'The monuments he constructed here were architecturally refined, with the intricate ornamentation we love so much. The mosaics, the blue-tiled domes, the breath-taking facades—we owe all of these to Temur.'

❅❅❅

Another such monument, the Registan, is just a short walk away. Meaning *sandy place,* this complex of three majestic madrasahs was built around a vast sandy courtyard to accommodate the camels, horses and donkeys of the Silk Road caravans. From our viewpoint on the upper terrace, the tableau is almost surreal, the dimensions incomprehensible.

Descending the stone staircase, we join the handful of visitors standing, ant-like, between the colossal mosque portals, each over thirty metres high. The brickwork is the colour of the desert sand and the walls seethe with a mass of complex designs, inscriptions and delicate swirling patterns in turquoise, emerald green and cobalt blue—a breathtaking combination of vastness and delicacy.

Ulugbek, the oldest madrasah, was built in the 15th century and was one of the leading universities in the Muslim world, and a centre for science. Sher-Dor was built two centuries later, its ornate portal featuring a pair of tigers looking out over the square from behind two rising suns. The clearly depicted human faces of the animals are an obvious breach of Islamic guidelines regarding figurative art, Yusuf explains, and an example of how Samarkand has always made up its own rules. The third madrasah, Tillya Kori, was built ten years later. With its richly-gilded mosque and galleries of student dormitories, it was, for a long time, one of the most important religious centres in the region. It is still the heart of the city, Yusuf says, functioning not only as a centre of spiritual teaching and worship, but also as a vibrant marketplace.

In its cavernous lower cells, artisans are at work creating marvellous artefacts. Merchants beckon to us, encouraging us to admire, compare and bargain, as they would have done centuries ago. It's good to arrive early, Yusuf recommends, as there is always a discount for the 'first sale of the day', which brings good luck to the merchant, and a bargain for the buyer.

❦❦❦

Beyond the Registan is a wide avenue lined with up-market stores, showcasing a tantalising array of quality garments, jewellery and ceramics. Many sell wedding attire. We are intrigued to see richly patterned traditional gowns displayed alongside strapless white meringue-dresses, and bejewelled caftans and turbans beside pin-striped morning suits and top hats.

At the far end of the avenue looms Bibi-Kanym, the oldest mosque in Samarkand. According to legend, Amir Temur is said to have commissioned hundreds of architects, painters and builders to construct this monumental edifice in honour of his favourite wife Bibi, while he went off on a campaign in 1399. It was to be the biggest building in the East, exceeding all mosques of the world with its size, proportions and beauty. When he returned five years later, it was ready and magnificent, with over three hundred marble columns supporting tapered arches and towering minarets at each end. In antiquity, its splendid blue dome was compared with the dome of Heaven, and the arched portal with the Milky Way. Unfortunately, soon after its completion, when it was fast becoming the popular place for ceremonial acts of worship, Bibi-Kanym began to collapse. Temur's ideas, it was said, were too bold for that period.

Wandering through the mosque now, such a premise is believable. The building's proportions are indeed humungous, with the walls and minarets sloping off in alarming directions. Some sections have toppled inwards and remain in ruins; even now it doesn't feel quite safe. But, despite the deep cracks in the brickwork, the broken lattice at the windows and the damaged or missing mosaics, the old 'Falling-Down Mosque' still exudes grandeur.

Hawkers won't leave us alone, so we escape back onto the avenue and walk to the end, where the land slopes away to the bustling Siob bazaar and the sea of cube houses spreading eastwards to the old city wall.

Yusuf suggests we eat lunch before tackling the market, and recommends a restaurant where we can sample the same meal that the great Tamerlane would have fed his troops, guaranteed to revive and fortify: a bowl of hearty corn soup, bread, and a portion of meat casseroled with apricots. The meal works its magic for Mark, Rae, Maz and Monika, who rush off to the market, but Larry and I, weary from the day's conquest thus far, return to the Golden Globe and our books.

Late in the afternoon, I walk around the corner to the internet café I had noticed earlier, on the first floor of a dishevelled building set below road-level. Out the front, a man is shovelling clay from the embankment into a wheelbarrow. When it's full, he pushes it past me and empties it onto the ground in an adjacent yard, where two other men are making bricks. One, old and bent, is throwing handfuls of straw onto the pile, while the other fills a row of metal moulds, patting the sludge down with his hands. Observing the lines of completed bricks drying in the sun, I'm impressed, but at the same time a little worried about the stability of the excavated roadway. The bank is scored with deep cracks, and rivulets of water have turned the footpath into a quagmire. Dodging muddy holes, I negotiate my way to an external staircase and climb to the top, where a large room is set up with bulky computers, surrounded by teenage boys drinking coca-cola and jostling for places.

A young man points to the price list on the wall—1,000UZS for one hour—then directs me to a smaller room, where younger boys are playing computer games.

While I wait for my machine to boot up I watch the antics of the boy beside me. He is playing a video game called *Terrorist*. It is predictably violent, like the games played by young people back home, except in this context, machine-gun-wielding soldiers are charging through walled compounds, mosques and bazaars, rather than futuristic cityscapes. Of course they are shooting at anything that moves and the blood splats are horribly realistic. The boy sees me watching and smiles, then, leaning over, he guides me through the icons on my computer screen to an English version of Google. I mutter my thanks, intrigued by this contradictory display of gentleness.

I check my emails, send a few to let people know that I am alive and well, then head back out, paying the boy by the exit desk. This session has cost me roughly 15 cents.

Back at the Globe, another picnic dinner is under way, thanks to my tour mates who have returned from the market with a bounty of cheese, bread, bananas, dates, dried lychees and pretzels. Rae presents another new cushion cover; Mark rolls his eyes but we all know he is secretly pleased. Monika has also made a purchase—a lovely suzani in subtle shades of blue and cream, for a bargain price, she claims. Maz confesses that her bartering session hadn't gone quite so well. She had expressed an interest in a handbag, but the initially-charming vendor had turned nasty when she didn't buy it. In her hurry to get away, she had been swallowed up by the crowd, unable to find the others, and had walked back to the hotel alone, a little unnerved by the whole experience.

We eat, then begin our habitual after-dinner card game, keeping an eye out for Nila and Tatyana, who are nowhere to be seen. It seems both couples have left in a hurry.

❦❦❦

The next day begins with another hearty breakfast in the courtyard: more fried eggs, salami, cheese, cherries, bread, and today's cake, layered with walnuts, spices and meringue.

Today is a 'free day' but we have asked Yusuf to organise a number of activities on our behalf.

He arrives in a mini bus which, to our surprise, drives right into the entrance foyer in between the TV set and the lounge, where yesterday's messenger boys are sitting, eyes glued to the screen. We're pleased to see the same driver, Mahmut, at the wheel. We climb in and he reverses back

53

out onto the street, turning away from the centre and plunging into the maze of back streets, where women are gossiping in doorways and men are ambling along the roadside, on their way to the local *hammam* (bathhouse), Yusuf suggests.

On the outskirts of the city, we stop at a large house surrounded by fruit trees and wild gardens. It is a silk carpet factory, run by an established family and renowned for the high quality of its hand-woven rugs and kilims. Alisher, the affable owner, comes out to greet us in the courtyard where huge vats of liquid are bubbling away over open fires.

'These vats contain the dyes for colouring the silk threads,' he explains. 'We use only natural dyes—pigments from walnut shells, pomegranate peels, asparagus stems and the leaves of indigo plants. So they will never fade.'

He points to three huge concrete tubs. 'After dying, the threads are rinsed in these baths, then hung to dry on the metal rails over there, by the entrance to the factory.'

'So, where are the silkworms?' Mike asks.

'This is the final stage of production,' Alisher answers. 'The silkworms are cultivated elsewhere,' he says. 'Once the worms start pupating, their cocoons are dissolved in boiling water, leaving the silk fibres behind. These are fed into a spinning reel and fused to make the threads we use here for carpet-making.' He passes around some samples, (each made up of over six hundred fibres), for us to examine, and test for strength.

Inside the house, we pass through a succession of light, airy rooms where young women are kneeling or crouching in rows on low platforms before huge wooden looms. Some are working alone, some in pairs.

'The weavers are chosen not only for their skill,' Alisher explains, 'but for their patience and dedication. They enjoy excellent conditions, generous wages and rewards for outstanding work. According to my family's philosophy, workers will be at their most productive when they are valued and happy.'

'A carpet is always woven by the same person or persons, from beginning to end,' he continues. 'Firstly the looms are strung with the backing threads, then the coloured fibres are knotted according to the designs, printed to a much reduced scale, on small pieces of paper.' (*Very* small pieces of paper we notice, pausing by a loom where a young woman is configuring an intricate border.)

'When the weaving is finished, the knots are torn and cut, usually by men, since it is such physically demanding work. Then the carpets are washed, dried in the sun, and stored here, in the display hall.'

Alisher indicates an ornate, carved doorway, inviting us to pass through and be seated. 'Welcome Tea' arrives, and as we sip from tiny gold-embossed cups, an array of beautiful carpets are laid out before us to admire, the colours and lustres taking on soft, silvery tones when they are rotated.

Rae asks the cost of a carpet.

'It will depend on the number of knots, the fineness of the thread and the intricacy of the design,' Alisher explains, 'but the prices are quite reasonable, considering that one carpet may take a year and a half to produce. Our carpets are made mainly on request, using traditional designs, but sometimes the purchaser has specific instructions. These carpets will be more expensive and must be paid for in advance,' he says, holding up a photograph of a carpet featuring a German Shepherd dog. 'As you can imagine,' he adds wryly, 'carpets such as these would be impossible to sell otherwise.' He admits that a handsome silk carpet is a luxury which cannot be afforded by everyone. 'But, they are in great demand,' he boasts, 'particularly in the Middle East.'

⁂

Our next destination is a silk paper factory in a small village not too far away. Driving through surprisingly verdant countryside, Yusuf tells us the story of paper-making, quoting the words of his hero, Navoi, who described paper as '… the wings that spread around the thoughts of wise men'.

Paper, he says, was invented by the Chinese in the early second century. Before that, scribes had written on bamboo, or pieces of silk. Silk was expensive and bamboo heavy, so neither of these materials was convenient. Ts'ai

Lun, an enterprising official of the Imperial Court had another idea. He began by breaking up the bark of a mulberry tree and pounding the fibres into a crude sheet. When he added rags, hemp and old fish nets to the pulp, his mulberry paper was much-improved and soon it was being widely used throughout China.

For centuries, the Chinese guarded their paper-making secrets to ensure a monopoly, but slowly, via the Silk Road, knowledge of its manufacture spread to the rest of world—firstly to the Xinjiang area, then to Tibet and India. In 751 A.D., when the T'ang army was defeated by the Ottoman Turks at a mighty battle in modern day Kyrgyzstan, some Chinese soldiers and paper makers were captured and put to work producing paper in Samarkand. Because of the city's strategic location on the Silk Road, Samarkand paper was soon in high demand and remained so until the Industrial Revolution made other papers more economical and accessible. But recently, UNESCO has intervened, fostering home industries like this one, to revive the all-but-forgotten art.

We pull up beside a rustic wooden cottage. The head of the family, Bil, comes out to greet us, leading us to a shady terrace where a table is set for tea, overlooking a small stream and a slowly-spinning mill wheel. We have just had tea at the carpet factory, but in Uzbekistan, one does not offend by refusing this drink of hospitality. Our host follows the custom of first cleansing the bowl by filling it with tea and discarding the contents, then refilling it, twice, and returning the contents to the pot each time to assist the brewing.

Over to our left, under a crude lean-to, a young man and woman are stripping the bark from thin mulberry branches, then cutting the wood into uniform lengths for feeding into the fire. Beside them, mulberry bark is simmering away in huge metal woks.

Inside the house the various rooms are dedicated to the different stages of paper-making. In the first, bark pulp and binding adhesives are pounded to a paste by timber pestles driven by the water wheel. In the next room, heavy stones are used to press the paste into sheets, which are then pegged up to dry in a third room. In the last room, the paper is graded, according to texture and colour, then packaged, ready for distribution.

In the factory shop, a range of hand-made paper products is on sale—notepads, envelopes, books, cards and paintings. My favourites are the miniatures depicting Oriental scenes. I can't resist buying one. It comes rolled and 'gift-wrapped' in a sheet of cork-coloured silk paper, tied with a strand of straw.

In the back yard, we survey the peaceful rural scene. The young man and woman from the lean-to are sitting together by the stream, rocking a baby in a cloth hammock strung between two trees. The water-wheel clicks reassuringly, bees buzz around a cluster of boxes by the vegetable patch, and smoke curls up from the chimney of the outdoor kitchen.

Just as we are saying our goodbyes, the school bus pulls up on the roadside and five small children tumble out. The cheeky boys run and chase each other, while the little girls in their cute pinafores hold hands and stand quietly, watching us. Mahmut sounds the horn and they break into shy smiles.

✦✦✦

Next on the agenda is a wine degustation, back in the city. The winery, housed in a splendidly-white classical building, is like a museum, with terracotta urns, old bottles, photographs and wine memorabilia on display. A centuries-old, gnarled grapevine grows up through the floor, creeping around the pillars towards the light well in the ceiling.

As we browse, the host and wine librarian, Nariman, relates the history of winemaking in this locality. Of course the story begins with a legend:

'In ancient times,' he says, 'a horde of Arab horsemen swept across the region then known as Sogdiana, towards the wonderful city of Marakand (Samarkand), destroying everything in its path. Flourishing gardens were trampled, villages burned to the ground, and most of the inhabitants killed, apart from the young men who were taken as slaves, and the young women as concubines. During this time of

59

great suffering, a miracle occurred—a magical vine with mysterious berries appeared. The survivors named the vine *Taifi*, which means *tribe* or *gender*. The vine thrived and from that day on, the juicy pink berries gave longevity, vivacity and strength to the people.'

The Taifi berries were, of course, grapes, and the villagers soon learned how to use them to make crude wines. Centuries later, in 1868, a Russian merchant named Dmitriy Filatov arrived in Samarkand and here, in this very building, founded the region's first winemaking enterprise. The wines, made from those same Taifi grapes, were unsophisticated, but nonetheless won many medals in world competitions. (Nariman takes a bottle from the shelf above his head, and points proudly to a row of silver and gold stickers.) Sixty years later, a Russian scientist named Michael Khovrenko joined the company, bringing with him the technical expertise necessary for producing vintage wines from Taifi and other local grape varieties, such as Shirin, Aleatiko and Liquor Kaberne.

In the handsome tasting room, eight tulip glasses have been arranged before each place on the heavy wooden table, each containing a finger-full of wine. We work our way systematically through a selection of dry red and white table wines, and fruity dessert wines. Only two of the table wines are to our taste, but the sweeter wines, we all agree, are quite good.

The brandies, matured for two and ten years respectively, are left until last. Despite their richness and velvety smoothness, I seem to be the only one drinking them. Such a waste! I pull out my water bottle and head off to find a discreet place to empty it. As I leave the table, Rae joins me, thinking I am off to find the toilet. We discover that we must go outside and down the street to use the facilities in a nearby eating house. This minor inconvenience turns out to be a most pleasing diversion—the Islamic décor in the restaurant's grand foyer and elegant salon could well be the most beautiful in the land.

Back in the tasting room, I siphon the remains of my ten-year-old brandy into my now-empty water bottle, while the others mill around finalising their purchases. Maz spies me and contributes her glassful, then Larry's, and we agree, why stop here? We drain Rae's glass and Mark's, then tuck the half-full bottle into my shoulder bag.

Needing food to soak up the alcohol, we buy 'package' lunches from a small café just around the corner—plastic tubs of yoghurt soup with rice and dill, and boxed noodles with meat and vegetables—then return to the hotel for an afternoon siesta.

Three hours later, Mahmut collects us for what Yusuf insists will be the highlight of the day, a Costume and Dance show at the El Morosi Theatre.

We are hoping for live music and traditional dance; what we get instead is a choreographed account of Uzbekistan's history, with the costumes, dance and music reflecting the various cultures which have over time influenced the region: Sogdian, Greek, Mongol, Turkish, Chinese and Arabic. The music is pre-recorded, but authentic, and the performances exceed all our expectations.

Afterwards in the dazzling white-on-white foyer, where opulent costumes are displayed in glass cases against a background of plaster filigree and sparkling crystal, we share a glass of champagne with the troupe—vibrant, young Samarkanders, de-robed, but still flushed and excited from the performance. A perfect finish to what we all agree has been a most memorable day!

Chapter 3

Nurata-Kyzylkum

In the morning we say goodbye to Miram and the staff at the Golden Globe and take off in our minibus to explore Nurata-Kyzylkum, a remote region in the far north-west of Uzbekistan, characterised by harsh desert and wild mountains. Yusuf and our driver, Hamid, are well-acquainted; they chat away in Russian as we exit suburban Samarkand, leaving the mosques, bazaars and bustling city traffic behind.

Small dusty towns line the highway with men standing around in groups, or lounging on raised daybeds beside the roadway. Donkeys and cows graze on the verge, makeshift stalls sell fruit and drinks, and small children interrupt their games to wave.

Gradually the terrain becomes more mountainous. We follow a wide river-bed, dry apart from a muddy trickle along its belly. Leaning out the window, I see trucks parked down there and crews of men shovelling silt into barrows, perhaps for the new highway being constructed up ahead.

Unexpectedly, Hamid turns off to the right. Apparently this is the 'short-cut', but we don't get far; a hundred metres on, the road is blocked by a concrete barrier. Hamid and Yusuf confer, then we follow other cars that are taking a detour—a rough track swinging wide of the barricade, skirting the steep slope. When the small, over-loaded van in front of us almost topples over, we decide to get out, leaving Hamid to continue on alone, with Yusuf standing up ahead, shouting directions. Hamid accelerates quickly, veers sharply to the left, then to the right, and thankfully makes it through, wheels spinning as he reconnects with level ground. Forever mindful of the TRIARJE dream, I question Yusuf about the road closure—surely there is a good reason. He dismisses my concerns; regardless of why it is blocked, we must go this way because it's quicker.

The road surface continues to deteriorate as we head further west. Hamid drives skilfully, lurching from side to side dodging the deep potholes, while trying at the same time to maintain a good speed. Goats and sheep dot the sun-bleached landscape, tended by shepherds in long pale robes, their heads veiled against the searing sun; the distant, purplish hills shimmer in the heat. We approach two figures on the roadside, a man carrying a slaughtered lamb over his shoulder and a small boy running along behind him. A woman is waiting by a white adobe hut, her long skirt and white headscarf billowing in the hot wind. A little further on, we pass a pair of carts, one piled high with hay and another with firewood, the plodding donkeys barely visible beneath their load. Then a village materialises, a dozen-or-so huts on either side of the road. We're grateful when Yusuf suggests we stop for tea.

The café is a collection of day-beds like the ones we saw

earlier on, arranged on a raised concrete slab and serviced by a rough kitchen, its rusted tin roof held in place with large stones. Imitating the other patrons, we remove our shoes and place them in a neat row before climbing up onto the platform, where cushions are positioned around the low table in the centre.

Delicious smells waft out from the bakery, as waiters emerge through a set of swinging doors, carrying trays piled with freshly baked *samsa* buns. Yusuf suggests we share one between two of us as they are very heavy. Ordering coffee is, as always, a risky business, but when it arrives it's good, and the pastries are scrumptious, stuffed with meat, tomato and onion, with clear juices running out onto the plate as we cut them open.

Afterwards, we line up outside the drop-toilet out the back, our noses covered with tissues as flies swarm and buzz. This will be our last stop, Yusuf announces; we are expected for lunch at our home-stay in Sentab. Surely it can't be too much further.

A row of mountains erupts on our left, and to the right the vast plains disappear into a bluish haze. This haze is, in fact, Lake Aydorkul, a hundred or so kilometres away, stretching from east to west as far as the eye can see. Road signs point to once-thriving fishing settlements, but now the area is largely uninhabited, Yusuf says. Even by the lake, the ground is arid; only hardy, hooved animals can survive there.

About twenty kilometres short of the township of Nurata, we stop. Yusuf talks on the telephone with a local guide, Islan. He will meet us at the turnoff and bring another vehicle, one more suitable for the final ascent up the mountain. We laugh nervously. This is not what we had expected.

When we reach the turnoff, Yusuf jumps out and greets Islan, who is waiting there, as promised. After a long, animated conversation, Yusuf announces that we will not need to change vehicles after all. We're not sure if this is good news or bad.

This road is even rougher than the highway. Hamid drives tentatively, taking directions from Islan in the front seat. We reach a village, a huddle of mud huts at the base of the mountains. Children are playing football in the bare school yard and women, gathered outside the shop, stare at us suspiciously. The road narrows and becomes steeper, winding its way precariously up the mountainside. A smashed car, the last motorised vehicle we will see, lies abandoned in a culvert.

Thirty agonising minutes later, the hamlet of Sentab appears, a handful of stone houses straddling both sides of a muddy stream coursing down between round grey boulders from the bare hills above. Yusuf points out a large house on the right, one of three sponsored by UNESCO, but not ours, he says. We reach a crude bridge and hold our breaths as we pass over. Hamid negotiates the last curve and slope, and we pull up under a canopy of lush grapevines beside our house—neat, whitewashed and trimmed with blue.

Our hosts Sergei and Muhlima rush out to welcome us, offering their hands as we climb down from our vehicle. Muhlima, a diminutive, nut-brown woman in an *ikat*-print trouser dress, headscarf and plastic scuffs, grabs The Leopard Print Luggage and carries it deftly down the stone stairs to the terrace. Then she takes us on a tour of the house, proudly pointing out the various rooms: to the right of the front door, the sunny dining room with its wall of small-paned windows looking across to the mountains; behind it, the fuschia-pink girls' bedroom, bare apart from four thin mattresses spaced evenly on the wooden floor; on the left hand side at the back, the boys' bedroom, with four more sleeping mats and the walls painted with quaint jungle scenes; and lastly, at the front, a small sleep-out for Yusuf and Hamid.

We ask Yusuf about the possibility of uni-sex bedroom arrangements. Muhlima doesn't seem to mind, so I offer to share the jungle room with Maz and Larry; Mark and Rae take the pink room with Monika. We dump our bags and return to the dining room for lunch, squeezing down the hallway, past a chipped 70's dressing table and an old, empty fridge. I go to plug my camera charger into the power socket, but Muhlima shakes her head. ... No power! She confesses, with a chuckle, that there has been none for five days now.

It's mid-afternoon and we're starving. Muhlima's daughter-

67

in-law, Sumaya, brings steaming bowls of broth, brimming with succulent chunks of goat's meat, potatoes, carrots and cabbage. We eat, sitting on cushions arranged in a circle around a bright cloth in the middle of the floor. There are rounds of home-baked bread, and salad vegetables fresh from the garden—all so full of flavour!

After lunch, a few in the group decide to go exploring. Yusuf and Hamid take a nap, and I laze on the day bed beneath the walnut tree, strategically placed to take full advantage of the view. Filtered light casts dappled patterns on my skin and leaves float gently down, coming to rest beside me on the bright suzani spread. After the chaos of the city, Sentab is a peaceful haven.

Sergei is standing in the garden. A large, powerful man, tanned and toughened by the Uzbek sunshine and the rigours of village life, he exudes an attitude of confidence and contentment as he surveys his kingdom. Wending his way between the tall plants, he inspects the various vegetables and fruits, adjusts some trellis, pulls out some dead foliage and checks the water hoses snaking up from the stream. He draws a bucket-full of water, empties it into the top of the free-standing wash basin, standing like a sentinel on the upper terrace, then disappears behind the house.

I contemplate taking a shower. I haven't yet had the opportunity to inspect the 'bathroom', so I climb down from the daybed and follow the stone path to where it stands in the shadows, beside the vegetable patch. After a tentative push, the door creaks open. Weak light enters through a small, high window, exposing the mud-brick walls, painted a pale blue. A piece of rubber hose extrudes from the roof, topped with a spray head, connected, I presume, to the same water supply that feeds the new flushing toilet a little further down the path. Underfoot, the concrete floor is inlaid with small stones and pieces of broken tile to form a rustic pattern, a feminine touch which transforms the otherwise crude utilitarian space. It's become quite cool, so I decide to postpone my ablutions until the following day after our hike up into the hills, when a cold splash might be welcome.

The wanderers return. We open a bottle of our Samarkand wine, and begin our customary game of cards, reclining on the daybed as the sun sets. Storm clouds, gathered on the horizon, begin to move our way. Then, just before dinner, it begins to sprinkle.

Gathering up our things, we file into the dining room where Sumaya has laid out a light meal of bread, boiled eggs, cheese, radishes, tomatoes and cucumber. Through the small panes we watch the approaching storm, lighting candles as the rain starts to pelt down. Thunder booms ever closer and lightning flashes, rendering the sheer rock precipices in shining silver. It's beautiful and frightening at the same time.

Then, through the noise of the storm, we hear shouting. It's Sergei, calling us outside to watch the stream, which has tripled in volume and is coursing down the hill, ripping out trees and threatening to take out the bridge. The noise from stones being washed down in the torrent is deafening. I go to stand closer, but Yusuf calls me back; minutes later the bank is engulfed by the angry, surging water. Hamid decides to take our vehicle back over to the other side just in case; we watch nervously as the tail-lights disappear across the bridge.

Back inside, we take to our beds, reading by torchlight as the rain continues to pour down. I dare not sleep until it stops.

⟨⟨⟨

Day breaks, clear and sunny. The waters have miraculously subsided, leaving behind a wild tangle of branches, marooned rocks and plastic bags. And the bridge has somehow survived.

Today we will hike high up into the hills, to villages even more isolated than Sentab. Bowls of milky white rice sweetened with swirls of black molasses are waiting for us in the dining room, as well as warm bread, yoghurt, mulberries and tea. Yusuf is keen to make an early start so we eat quickly then set off, taking the path up the incline, away from the stream, between the dry-stone walls and vegetable gardens of the village houses. A herd of goats rushes up behind us, driven along by a man on a donkey; we quickly form a single line to let them pass. Yusuf calls out to the goatherd in Tajik and he grins a toothless smile. Another donkey follows bearing a young woman, riding side-saddle, nursing a small baby. She leads a third beast laden with baskets, blankets and bulging saddle bags. We follow this small family on the move to where the path re-connects with the stream in a steep-sided gully. The remains of a bridge tumbles into the water, a mess of twisted metal and concrete, and on the opposite bank, a small hut crouches on a narrow, grassy verge surrounded by garden beds. Yusuf explains that decades ago many people lived self-sufficient lives, tending their herds and farming these small fertile strips.

Many things changed during the Soviet era, he says. Uzbekistan was rich in resources, so the country's rural economy and traditional culture fell prey to rapid industrialisation, as large factories and manufacturing plants sprang up, invasive mining operations began, and agriculture was geared to produce cotton for the Soviet market. People left the crippled villages and found work in the emerging towns and re-constructed cities.

But now, the government is encouraging families to return to the countryside, to once more farm the land and to revive the traditional crafts. Homestay projects, like ours in Sentab, have been subsidised to promote tourism and stimulate employment.

Yusuf stops, pointing to a few crude figures etched into the bedrock. 'Petroglyphs,' he says. 'All of our history is embedded here, in these rocks. There are paintings of hunting rituals and battle scenes, of extinct and

71

domesticated animals, of weapons and religious symbols.'

'And there are more up here along the creek-bed,' he calls out, as he climbs onto a rock ledge. We start to follow, but he is already turning back. After the storm, the water is too high.

The path continues upwards. Far off to the right we spot a cluster of huts. A man on a horse approaches us from that direction, arriving at a fork in the track just as we do. 'He must be a wealthy man,' Yusuf comments after he has passed, on account of the horse, we presume.

We take the track to the left, leading diagonally upwards to the ridge. Rae calls out, pointing to sure-footed goats nibbling tufts of grass halfway up the steep cliff face, and soon after we reach a well-maintained house, tucked into a cleft. A big, fluffy dog runs to the fence and barks, trying to sound fierce; another continues to lie sunning itself in the narrow yard. A donkey neighs, poking its head out of a stone pen, laid meticulously in a herringbone pattern. We feed the curious animal some grass, patting its nose and talking to it as the little goats come clambering down to us, drawn perhaps by our voices, but more likely by the promise of food. There doesn't seem to be anyone about. We're surprised to see an electricity cable, threading its way up through the pass, connecting with this house, then continuing up to where a few more totter on the peak.

Three men are working up there on a raised platform, repairing the crumbling walls of the largest house and adding a new wing, laying stones in overlapping layers and securing them with mud. They look up and nod as we approach. Beside the house is a stack of metal roofing sheets. *However could they have gotten up here, I wonder?* Away to the left, smoke billows out from a humpy, half-buried in the hillside. A woman with a child on her hip watches us from behind a heavy blanket strung across its entrance. We wave, but she quickly disappears inside. More ruined houses spill down the rocky slope; we peer into windows and doorways, but the only inhabitants, apart from the family in the ridge house, seem to be donkeys.

On the next rise we lie flat on the rocks, peering down over another valley. To the right, a quarry lies abandoned; to the left, the stream winds its way past a puzzling arrangement of concrete blocks, resembling the foundations of some vast complex. Yusuf, joins us, too late to surprise us with what we have already discovered—the remains of a resort spa built by the Russians in the 60's, with roman-style baths, a cinema, and luxury accommodation for wealthy merchants and military officers. When the Soviet occupation ended, the buildings were apparently de-constructed, brick by brick, by the villagers, and used to build new houses and yards.

Two small donkeys follow us back to the ridge, watching curiously as we begin our descent. It's almost midday and we are expected back at the house for lunch at one-thirty, so we set a good pace, stopping only once to inspect the creek-bed petroglyphs, visible now that the water level has dropped. The images, painted in white ochre on the coal-black rock, are well-formed and distinct, depicting spears and axes, horses, camels, deer (or perhaps goats) and various clan symbols.

Back at the house, we collapse on the daybed, then take turns in the shower. Sumaya brings lunch—flatbread, white cheese, salad and fruit.

Gathering the plates together, Muhlima announces that tonight's dinner will be plov, and asks if we would like to watch her prepare it. Rae, Bronwyn and I jump at the opportunity.

We follow her to the outdoor kitchen, made of stones and mud—an amazing feat of engineering. The door and window apertures face the sheltered path to the left of the house, while another opening channels the breeze up from the valley, forcing the smoke from the cooking fires out through holes in the roof. The ovens are also made from rendered mud, with round holes in the top fashioned to fit the shapes of the various pots and pans.

Muhlima takes a giant wok and places it over the largest hole, stoking up the fire in the pit beneath. Reaching up, she chooses a ladle from a collection of implements hanging overhead and fills it with oil from a nearby crock. At just the right moment she drizzles it into the pan, then adds adds generous chunks of goat's meat, filling the room with delicious aromas.

She says she has been learning English and brings out a battered folder covered in brown paper, the stained pages filled with hand-written words. While the meat browns, she tells us about her family and her life in the mountains.

She holds up ten fingers, one for each of her children, nine boys and one girl. 'They are all grown up,' she says. Only her youngest son, eighteen-year-old Arkin, lives here with them now. Her daughter, Cyra, is married and lives in a nearby town with her husband's family. Another son, Ganwar, is working in Bukhara; his wife *was* living here with the family, but she has apparently 'run off'. (At this point, Muhlima pauses, removing the gelatinous meat to a platter and adding a huge pile of yellow carrots, cut into sticks. She spreads the fire to lower the heat and while the carrots stew, she resumes her story.) Her third son works in Nurata and is married to Sumaya, who lives here and helps in the house.

'We are very lucky to have her,' Muhlima says. 'It's very hard to look after the family and the guests, with only one daughter.'

Sumaya, busily filling a metal bucket from the tank in the corner, nods her head and looks pleased. She takes six handfuls of rice from a nearby sack, washes it once, twice, three times, then piles it on top of the glistening, softened carrots. Muhlima uses the end of a wooden spoon to poke steam holes in the mound before arranging the fragrant meat on top. Lastly she covers the wok with a broad lid. She checks the fire, now just a glow of embers, and announces that in three hours it will be done.

Back in the house, there is some excitement. The power has come on! We rush to plug in phones, cameras and lap-tops.

Suddenly it seems incredibly self-indulgent.

Accustomed now to completing tasks before nightfall, we pack our bags, ready for an early departure in the morning. Then, back outside on the day-bed, shot glasses of Samarkand brandy are distributed, and the pre-dinner card game begins. The sun sets behind the mountains in a cloudless sky, and just as darkness is closing in, the plov arrives.

It is brilliant, our best plov so far; the meat succulent and rich, the rice plump and savoury. It is amazing that such flavours can be achieved without the addition of stock, herbs or spices. When we tell Muhlima how good it is, she blushes like a school-girl. I ask if I can take her photo standing beside the plov pot. She agrees and surprises us all by undoing her headscarf and shaking out a long mane of charcoal-grey hair. She twists it back up into a neater knot, reties her scarf and then poses sternly for the camera; it is only when I bring up her image on the screen that she breaks into a smile.

❦❦❦

Our morning farewells are warm but reserved; physical contact in strange lands can be tricky.

Hamid has brought the car back over the bridge and we go

to collect our bags. I try to get a candid photo of Sergei carrying The Leopard Print Luggage, but he spots the camera and stops to pose, looking self-conscious.

The drive back down the mountainside seems less hazardous than our daunting ascent two days before; something to do with the familiar and the unknown, I guess. Back at the highway we turn to the left in the direction of Bukhara, and enter the Navoi region.

Archaeological excavations show evidence of settlement here some 40,000 years ago, Yusuf says. Legend has it that many millennia ago, a fire rock fell from the sky and a spring appeared where the meteorite had hit the ground. Since then a bounteous stream of water has bubbled up through the parched earth, sometimes taking on a strange radiance which the people call *Nur*, the *Ray from Allah*. The town of Nurata, named after the ray, grew up around the spring and believers came from neighbouring towns and beyond, to visit the well and the holy spring, and to bathe in the healing waters. In time, a mosque complex named Chasma (the Tadjik word for *spring*), was built in the town and it remains one of the most important Islamic centres in this area.

Hamid drops us at the entrance and we join the queue of worshippers filing through the exquisite mosaic portal into the vast paved square beyond.

The pretty Djuma Mosque on the left is open only to believers, so we head straight towards the ring of people peering into the well, the source of the mythical Chasma spring. A man in traditional dress (a long white *kuilak* shirt over loose trousers and a colourful turban) is recording the details of visiting groups in a clip folder. Yusuf, I notice, passes him money.

The well itself, surrounded by a low rock wall, is unremarkable, but the huge pond beside it, fed by the spring, is astonishing. The clear, bright-blue water is teeming with thousands of wonderful silver fish called *marinka*. They are scale-less and inhabit the waters of the pond and the underground channels that run below the town. Like the spring, they are considered to be sacred and are not eaten. We are amazed to learn that the water mysteriously maintains a constant temperature of 19.5 degrees Celsius, and does indeed contain micro-elements with healing qualities, as well as traces of gold, silver and bromide.

Behind the mosque complex, on a bald orange hill, are the remains of the ancient fortress of *Nur*, founded in the 4th century BC by Alexander the Great. Camels are ferrying visitors back and forth over the lower slopes, and people are clustered around the souvenir stalls that line both sides of the path that leads ultimately to the summit. Only a handful of pilgrims are braving the final section; it seems obligatory that we join them. There are no handrails or steps, and a strong wind whips around us as we shuffle along, clinging on to the weathered segments of Alexander's wall. Finally at the top, we can look down over the whole Chasma complex, the sprawling town, and the dusty, treeless plains beyond. What a vantage point!

Back at the base, we browse in the stalls, bursting with 'evil eye' trinkets and religious frippery. A number of stall holders are selling cute little bird whistles made from clay, and the air is full of chirruping and warbling. They're irresistible; the vendor shows me how to add water into the base, a little at a time, to achieve the perfect pitch.

Nearby, we find Hamid and Yusuf chatting to Muhlima's son, Furkat, who works here as a guide. He is on his break and can join us for lunch.

We are delighted to find that our restaurant is located in a communal park. Outdoor tables, day-beds and barbeques have been set up around a central kitchen, and waiters are ferrying loaded plates of food to families picnicking on the grass. We eat an excellent lunch of *shurpa* (a clear broth with meat, parsnip and herbs), an assortment of kebabs (including a delicious kidney and pimento combination), and a selection of salads.

Afterwards, we girls go off to the 'rest rooms' on the other side of the park. Waiting in line beneath a frangipani tree, we watch a young woman embroidering a suzani cloth, her dark eyes flashing beneath a single charcoaled eyebrow. When we admire her work, her shy smile reveals more of those gleaming, gold-capped teeth.

Hamid brings the bus. We pass through the quiet town, then plunge back into the desert.

Being one of only two double-land-locked countries in the world (the other is Lichtenstein), Uzbekistan's climate is naturally harsh, but mismanagement and disregard for the environment have made things significantly worse, Yusuf says. More than eighty-five percent of the land now suffers desert or semi-desert conditions. During the Soviet era, the hunger for water resources resulted in the drying of the Aral Sea and the Amu Darya River, causing disastrous and far-reaching damage to the eco-system. The region's once prosperous fishing industry was all-but destroyed, bringing unemployment and economic hardship to the lake communities, while the surrounding lands were irreparably degraded through soil salinization, erosion, unsustainable agricultural practices and mineral exploitation. Traversing this monotonous landscape of sand dunes, dromedaries, camels and yurts, we are lulled into a half-sleep.

Suddenly Yusuf jumps up, shouting for Hamid to stop. He climbs out and retrieves a Russian tortoise from the middle of the road, its arms and legs flailing about, its neck extended, and its scared, beady eyes darting. Yusuf says if we're lucky we might also see a giant monitor lizard, a saiga antelope, a wild boar, or a Turkestan pheasant. They're obviously hiding, or are too well camouflaged, for all we spot is a golden eagle, a few mining rigs and an aluminium smelter way off in the distance.

❦❦❦

Chapter 4

Bukhara

The Bukhara region has been inhabited for at least five millennia and the ancient city of Bukhara is believed to have existed for at least half of that time. One of the oldest cities along the Silk Road, it was a hub of trade, scholarship, culture and religion.

We are thrilled to learn that our guesthouse, Mekhtar Ambar, was once a caravanserai. Its entrance in Nakshbandi Street is clandestine—a single doorway in an unadorned brick wall—but when the heavy wooden doors swing open, an octagonal courtyard is revealed (where camels and horses would once have been fed and watered), surrounded by a series of rooms accessed through ornate archways. The downstairs rooms house the reception office, kitchen, dining room and staff quarters, and upstairs are the guest bedrooms, opening onto a mezzanine terrace. I have first choice of two single rooms: one small and charming with soaring white-washed ceiling arches and its own ensuite; the other much larger, but with an external bathroom. I take the second—with its latticed windows, wooden ceiling, lacquered furniture and suzani wall hangings, it is instantly appealing.

We're pretty tired from the day's journey, so we opt for another courtyard dinner and card game. Rae and I go off to

shop, and in a store close by we find everything we need—
Bukhara bread (soft and light and sprinkled with bitter
black seeds), goat's cheese, a spicy lamb sausage, sweet
date biscuits, speckled apricots, and tiny sugar bananas.

Yasmin, the receptionist, brings plates, glasses and cutlery
to the table on the upper terrace, now bathed in the soft
orange hues of sunset. Over a few more bottles of
Samarkand wine, the Mark-Richelle-Monika team scores
another victory.

❦❦❦

Breakfast at Mekhtar Ambar is a real treat. The dining
room is a delight in itself, with its chalky white walls,
arched ceilings, recessed shelves displaying artefacts, and
walls hung with embroidered cloths and ceramic platters.
Our table awaits us on our first morning, set with the
traditional blue and white crockery and standard
accompaniments—pots of black and green tea, dishes of
honey, baskets of warm bread, bowls of sliced cucumber
and slabs of white cheese. Yasmin brings fried eggs, *manti*
dumplings stuffed with meat, and finally, chunks of juicy
pink watermelon.

Yusuf appears later in the foyer, looking rather unkempt;
we suspect he may have bedded down in the office last
night. Regardless, he is his usual cheerful self, and we head

off on foot down Nakshbandi Street towards the domes and minarets of the centre.

Our first stop is Lab-i Hauz, a mosque complex set around a sixteen-metre-deep rectangular pond. Bukhara was once watered by a network of canals feeding into some two hundred stone pools; they were the city's principal source of water and the place where people gathered and gossiped, drank and washed. Not surprisingly, plagues were common and during the '20s and '30s most were filled in by the Soviets. Lab-i Hauz, meaning *by the pond,* is one of only a few to have survived. It's quite picturesque, with ducks swimming around a miniature floating castle in the centre, and a five-hundred-year-old mulberry tree overhanging it on one side.

We assemble in the square, raised up above the pond on the northern side, in front of the largest madrasah in the city, also named Kukeldash, like the one in Tashkent. From here we can look across to the sumptuous Khanaka (a lodging-house for itinerant Sufis), and the Nadir Divan-Beghi Madrasah, its portal adorned with a sparkling mosaic phoenix.

An affable, roly-poly man approaches us, dressed in a red tunic and elaborate tasselled hat, peddling water from a bloated pig-skin bag. Vying for attention, a wizened gypsy woman pushes him away, setting his metal cups clinking and clanging while she swings her incense thurible, boldly lifting our skirts and calling out incantations in her shrill voice, promising to drive out evil spirits. Embarrassed, Yusuf steers us towards a life-sized brass statue of a man riding a donkey.

'This is Efendi,' he explains, 'a legendary joker who taught wisdom through his telling of irreverent fables, poking fun at the rich and haughty.' He is obviously a popular figure— visitors are lining up to have their photos taken with him.

Kulkedash is typically ornate and constructed in the standard madrasah configuration, with tall minarets flanking the main entrance portal. Inside, merchants and artisans are setting up their stalls around the perimeter of the internal courtyard. Rae and Maz engage in some hard bargaining for embroidered handbags and cushion covers while I rifle through a pile of colourful, beaded tassels like the ones decorating the entrance to the dining room of our hotel. Yasmin told me that they are made by the Bedouins, to embellish the women's' costumes and decorate the doorways of their tents. I can imagine a set hanging either side of my living room mantelpiece. The jewellery is interesting too. Many of the pieces are set with semi-precious stones and dark-orange coral from the Black Sea and different to what we've seen in Uzbekistan so far. 'These are from Iran,' one stall-holder explains. 'They are very old.' I'm tempted, but I do already have a few pendants like this, bought in Turkey a few years ago, for a fraction of the price.

A short distance from Kulkedash is the entrance to what was once one of the most colourful and cosmopolitan trading centres in the Islamic world, comprising five vaulted and domed *toks* or bazaars, each monopolising separate trades. From dawn to dusk an endless procession of donkeys, camels and carts coursed their way through this maze of laneways, laden with treasures from far-away lands. Arabian horses, tethered in the caravanserais were bought, sold and traded, tea houses seethed with merchants, moneylenders struck deals with secret handshakes or ring imprints in wax, and a small army of shaslik-sellers, bakers, blacksmiths and barbers rushed to and fro, catering to every need.

Only three of the five toks have survived the march of time. Tok-i-Zargaron is one of them. Its speciality was jewellery, handcrafted in gold, silver, coral and precious stones, but today the range of merchandise includes embroidered costumes, hand-painted wooden boxes, ceramic platters and embossed metal goods.

Music lures us outside to where a man is playing an intriguing, long-necked lute. '*Rubob*,' he explains, finishing the phrase and returning the instrument to its place on the benchtop of his stall, alongside a dozen others. '*Tanbur, tor, dutor*,' he continues, pointing to those with strings. Next he takes up a bamboo *nah*, and blows into it, producing a sweet, flute-like tone, then a *karnay*, sounding more like a muted trumpet. Lastly he selects a *ng'ora* drum, entertaining us with a series of deft clicks and riffs. We applaud loudly and buy copies of his CD, featuring many of these instruments and the National Symphony Orchestra of Uzbekistan.

Just behind his stall is the Zargaran mosque, its carved

portal weathered and crumbling. Centuries ago, busy merchants would have ducked in here for prayers, without having to waste too much haggling time. More recently, it's been converted to a cool, damp gallery. Stained arched ceilings soar above our heads and wonderful antique carpets and rugs cover the stone walls and the uneven flagstones. But it's the paintings that draw us in—portraits of wizened traders, lively market scenes and evocative madrasahs.

Yusuf leads us on to a metal workshop in the next street, where we pause to watch a young man etching decorative designs onto the blades of small knives with an electric engraving tool, sparks flying in all directions. He works three-at-a-time, carving them, dipping them in acid, polishing them with a cloth, then laying them beside the others in a neat, shining row. The shop's interior is like a museum, with old swords, knives, bowls and platters mounted on the dark walls. We are offered tea, but Yusuf declines, pointing to his watch and herding us along to the next building, Bozori Kord Hammam, an historic bathhouse.

A memorable hammam experience in Turkey a few years ago has left me hankering for more, so when Yusuf says this one comes highly recommended, I don't need to be won over. Monika is keen too, but the others are undecided. Right now, it's closed, so we will have to return later.

The row of stalls along the busy street continues, displaying a seemingly endless array of merchandise: saddles and bridles, animal skins, ropes and string, ceramics and gourds. The large ones, we are told, are for holding water, the smaller ones for tea, and the tiny ones for spices.

Right at the end is Abdullah Khan Tim, the second surviving bazaar, once the most elegant trading hall in Bukhara, where silk and wool was sold by Afghan traders, instantly recognisable by the tail of silk that trailed from the left side of their turbans. Today, dressmakers still source their fabrics here and continue to sew exquisite costumes in their workshops. Yusuf leads us into a cavernous hall—for tea, he says. Sure enough, on a raised platform in one corner, there are tables set with patterned china and bejewelled, crown-shaped tea cosies. As we sip fragrant tea spiced with cardamom and nibble on squares of chewy sesame-and-nut toffee, Ramil, the proprietor, gives us the run-down on his merchandise, laying out before us, bolts of bright cottons and silks, gorgeous scarves and intricately embroidered suzanis. Most of his wares are antiques, he says, not just from Uzbekistan but also from neighbouring Kazakhstan, Tajikistan and Turkmenistan.

The last surviving tok is the Cap-Makers' Bazaar, a wheel-like structure with the tomb of holy-man, Khoia Ahmed I Paran, in the centre, allegedly bringing good fortune to the traders whose stalls line the narrow corridors running off it like irregular spokes. True to its name, we find whole walls of tiubitekas: plain, embroidered, round, square, black, coloured, tassled, silk, velvet, cotton and woollen. Some are antiques, but many of the caps are new, made by resident embroiderers and milliners working away in their dimly-lit cells.

It's lunchtime. We leave the market and enter a dark alleyway, lined with ramshackle warehouses. Yusuf leads us through the low doorway of one such building, then up and up, through three floors of rickety rooms to a rooftop *restoran* perched high above Po-i Kalyan Square, with a bird's eye view of the 14th century Kalyan mosque and the great Kalyan minaret, with its iconic bands of glazed blue tiles.

Yusuf relates the minaret's legendary story:

In 1127, the ruler, Arslan Khan, killed a holy imam. Afterwards the imam's spirit came to him in a dream, asking that his head be laid in a place where nobody could tread on it. The khan thus decreed that this forty-five-metre-high brick tower be built over his grave, and from the arched fenestrations of its rotunda, the Muslims of the city were called every day to prayer. (Kalyan was also dubbed the Tower of Death, because for centuries, criminals, including women accused of adultery, were tossed off the top onto the stone of the square below.)

We turn our attention from the vista to the tabletop, set with rustic terracotta crockery. The menu predictably features shasliks, but these are made from minced lamb and doused with lemon and fresh mint. The salads—cucumber raita, tomato-and-watermelon salsa and beetroot-and-carrot slaw—are different too, and equally delicious. We linger over the meal, appreciating the cool ambience of the terrace.

Yusuf reminds us that we still have many wonderful things to see. Retracing our footsteps, we return to the square, then branch off to the right, following an alley lined with small shops selling domestic goods and mercery. I want to buy a trouser-dress, like so many of the women wear, but they are nowhere to be found. Yusuf is no help. 'Women's business,' he jokes. We do find shops selling lengths of the bright ikat fabric. Perhaps the dresses are made to order.

Our next destination is the Ark, a sprawling earthen fortress dating back to the 5th Century AD, set apart from the bazaars on a huge tract of barren ground. The sun beats down relentlessly as we follow its solid sloping walls, interspersed with a series of perfectly aligned, conical pillars.

According to legend, the epic hero Siyavusha was responsible for creating this massive edifice. As a young man, he fell in love with the daughter of the local ruler, Afrosiaba, who set him the seemingly impossible task of building a palace in the area covered by a bull's skin. Clever Siyavusha cut a hide into narrow strips, joined the ends together and proceeded to construct the Ark within its boundaries, thus gaining Afrosiaba's permission to marry. Siyavusha was later accused of plotting to overthrow the king and was subsequently executed in front of his wife.

Historical records, on the other hand, indicate that it was a ruler named Biden who built the original Ark. Many times it was destroyed and many times rebuilt, until wise men advised that it should be constructed around seven points, as in the constellation of Ursa Major (The Great Bear). Rebuilt in this fashion, it was never again destroyed.

Apart from housing a succession of royal families, the Ark was an unrivalled centre of culture and learning. Yusuf quotes Avicenna, the 10th century Persian philosopher and scientist, who wrote: 'I found (in the library of the citadel) such books, about which I had not known and which I had

never before seen in my life. I read them, and I came to know each scientist and each science. Before me lay gates of inspiration into great depths of knowledge which I had not surmised to exist'.

Unfortunately, this great legacy was lost over centuries of conquests, the last being led by the Bolsheviks in 1920. During the Siege of Bukhara, the Ark was bombed and much of the structure remains in ruins. It is believed that the last Emir, Alim Khan, who escaped to Afghanistan with the royal treasury, actually ordered the Ark to be blown up, so that its secret places (especially the harem) could not be desecrated.

The entrance is barricaded and shrouded in muslin—it seems that the stone wall on the left has collapsed and visitors cannot enter due to repairs and renovations. We stand in the forecourt looking up at the twin towers framing the winched ramp which leads up to the gateway; beyond, Yusuf says, are the remains of the mint, the temples, the barracks, the offices, the warehouses, the workshops and the stables which made up the citadel. (I dare not mention the names Charles Stoddart and Arthur Connolly, the British officers who were caught up in the 19th century Anglo-Russian struggle for dominance in Central Asia, or the film *The Great Game* which documents how they were held prisoner here in a vermin-infested pit for two years by the Emir, before being publicly beheaded and buried somewhere under the square outside the main gate.) I suggest we move on, and quickly.

We cross to the 'Old Mother' mosque opposite, defined by the massive, wooden pillars which support its soaring portico, the once-bright hues now faded and weathered. Inside, the moss-green carpet is printed with rows of gold, prayer-rug-size rectangles, but the space is glaringly devoid of worshippers. It suddenly occurs to me that throughout Uzbekistan we've seen little evidence of the actual practice of Islam.

When questioned, Yusuf makes blanket references to the government's policy of religious tolerance, and the concept of 'Islam by Choice'. Rumour has it that after an initial resurgence in Islam following Independence, the people (now significantly poorer) may be turning away from Islam. Also, on a more sinister note, that the government may be actively discouraging its practice, by closing mosques, and banning attendance at prayer and the observation of Ramadan. On reflection, I haven't once heard the *azon*, the call to prayer, as it is known here.

Regardless, mosques, madrasahs and mausoleums abound. Wandering through the streets of the old town, one simply 'encounters' them, intermingled with the ordinary houses. Some are restored but most exist and function in a state of partial decay. It is here, Yusuf suggests, that one may find the faithful, worshipping discreetly.

I've had more than enough sight-seeing for one day, but Yusuf has other ideas. We must still visit Sitora-I-Mohi-Hosa, the Summer Palace of Emir Ahadhan, on the outskirts of the city. At least we don't have to walk. Yusuf hails two taxis and negotiates a return fare. It's quite a way, back along the road to Nurata. The drivers, who will wait for us, light up cigarettes and lounge against the fence under a tree as we file in past the sentry box.

Ahadhan, we are told, built this extravagant retreat in 1911, following a visit to St Petersburg, precipitating a curious blend of Russian and Uzbek architecture. We tramp from room to room, a little overwhelmed by the obscene grandeur, finally exiting into the palace grounds, where we take tea in a small cafe beside the garish harem quarter.

Pointing to a nearby tower, Yusuf relates how the emir liked to gaze upon his concubines from above, as they wandered freely between the sumptuous rose-beds. His pleasures were, however, short-lived: he and his entourage were forced to flee in the face of the Russian Revolution. The Bolsheviks spared the palace (no doubt due to its original links with Russia) and used it as a kidney hospital, but after the Revolution it fell quickly into disrepair. Like many of the country's historic monuments, it is now being restored. Sitting in the dusty yard sipping green tea beside an Olá ice-cream cart with loud techno music blasting out from a beat box, it's hard to imagine this by-gone world of decadence.

When we finally arrive back at the caravanserai, we are disappointed to see two young women sitting at *our* table on the upper terrace. Sipping pale-pink liquid from tall-necked bottles and lacquering their nails, they look very much like typical Western girls getting ready for a big night out. We retreat to my room for refreshments, congregating around the low coffee table, imagining the cool breeze outside.

Thirty minutes later, the girls are still gossiping and giggling in our corner. Winking back at the others, I approach them, armed with a wine bottle and a cheese plate, and ask if we might join them. They agree immediately, shuffling up to the far end of the table, but soon make their excuses and move off to their rooms to put the finishing touches to their outfits.

❦❦❦

Our last day in Bukhara is blissfully free, apart from dinner and a show in the evening.

Over breakfast, we put together an itinerary of sorts, beginning with a return to Kulkedash to shop for gifts.

By 10 a.m. the market stalls are well and truly set up, with stallholders spruiking their 'first sale of the day' offers. We bargain hard and get some great deals on embroidered handbags, fancy slippers with turned-up toes, and tiubiteka skull caps. I go off to look for wedding tassels, and find the perfect pair made from black wool interwoven with indigo beads and silver amulets. We meet back by the entrance, where a clever calligrapher is demonstrating his ancient craft, using angled brushes of fine horse-hair to create florid artworks in Arabic script.

Next, we return to Borzi Kord. This time the heavy wooden doors of the hammam are open. Monika and I each book a massage for one o'clock and after some gentle persuasion, Maz and Larry decide to try one too. They take the last available session at eleven-thirty, just fifteen minutes away. The rest of us continue along Halim Ibodov Street to the highly-recommended Silk Road Spices Tea House.

Despite the oppressive humidity, the interior of the *chaikhana* is surprisingly cool and inviting. Candles flicker in wall sconces, illuminating the low stone ceiling and carpet-clad walls, music plays unobtrusively in the background, and the air is tinged with the tantalising aromas of coffee and spices.

A handsome young man dressed in loose printed trousers and a white caftan over-shirt, leads us to a daybed in a far corner. Removing our shoes, we clamber up, sinking back

94

into the cushions. Our host, whom we suspect may be the son of Mirfayz Ubaydov (the famous Bukhara spice merchant who runs this establishment), explains that for 11,000 UZS per person we can sample a selection of exotic beverages and sweets.

We indulge ourselves with pots of tea flavoured with cloves, ginger and saffron, and the Silk Road's 'special blend' coffee (a divine brew infused with cardamom and rose water). Small plates of crunchy sesame balls, bite-size pieces of bitter nut-toffee, and tiny squares of halva complete the extravagance.

Time stands still.

When we finally emerge into the full blaze of the hot midday sunshine, we collide with Larry and Maz, fresh and glowing from the hammam. I must admit, I'd been a little worried about how Maz would cope, but her elated grin says it all.

Monika and I are excited now and head back to Borzi Kord, where we surrender to the attention of Arkin, the young man who seems to be in charge. Despite his youth, he is commanding. Clad in just a white towel tied at his narrow hips, he ushers us towards the dressing cubicles where we exchange our street clothes for cotton wraps and towelling scuffs. Then we follow him into the labyrinth of damp 14th century corridors, past cavern-like spaces set with stone tables. Weak light filters in through pin-hole cavities in the vaulted roof and cool water trickles along shallow channels beside the walls. It feels ancient and decadent.

We stop in a steam room, and Arkin speaks for the first time. 'Please, you will lie here.' With that, he pads off, his lithe, muscled body disappearing into the void.

Monika and I take our places on opposite sides of the room, easing ourselves down onto the hard stone benches. Breathing deeply, I extend my backbone and try to relax my muscles, one by one. When I glance over at Monika, I see that she is stretching too. It's getting hot now, and steamy. The cotton wrap is clinging to my sweating body and rivulets of perspiration are running from my forehead down the side of my face and neck and dripping onto the stone. I try to visualise the toxins seeping out through my pores, cleansing and purifying, but instead I'm beginning to panic. I don't know how much longer I can last.

Sensing movement, I open my eyes and see that Arkin has come for Monika, leaving me alone, without a word. More deep breaths…

Finally Arkin re-appears, his handsome face next to mine. Taking my hand, he raises me up and leads me to a dusky chamber, where his strong but gentle hands begin their magic.

My wrap dissolves and my body, slippery with oil, feels like rubber as it is kneaded, twisted, cracked and eased into the most unnatural postures. Neck, shoulders, arms, back, buttocks, legs… Then he rolls me over, his slender fingers intertwined with mine. Our eyes lock for a brief moment before he moves on to feet, ankles, thighs, abdomen, belly, chest... In this strange, erotic, massage-world I am a goddess, my yielding body worshipped and adored. I want this to go on forever, but eventually the stroking becomes less urgent, more like a caress, the lingering kiss of a lover.

'Are you ok?' Arkin whispers. Fantasy over, I feel almost embarrassed, but he seems relaxed and composed. With his hand on my belly, he fingers the gold ring at my navel and asks, 'Was it good?'

I nod, a little self-consciously. But from the softness in his dark eyes I can see that he is genuinely curious.

'Mm,' I reply, nodding and smiling a little wickedly.

Handing me my wrap, he helps to fasten it around my chest and shepherds me towards the shower room. Standing beneath the sublimely cool stream of water, I run my hands proudly over my body, remembering Maz's secret smile earlier in the alleyway.

Back in the foyer, Arkin and his assistant (Monika's masseur) are preparing herbal tea. In our fresh dry sarongs, wet hair twisted up, we share this formality, sitting opposite each other at the oversized antique table. After the intimacy of the massage, it seems surreal. Feigning composure, I ply Arkin with questions. He confirms that he is a hammam master, having completed seven rigorous years of training in this unique branch of Oriental massage. He is proud to be part of this tradition.

A bell sounds, signalling the arrival of another client group. Monika and I quickly dress, say our goodbyes and return to the chaos of the bazaar, so much more bearable now.

⬥⬥⬥

Back at the hotel there is little time to languish. At five o'clock we must make our way to the Nadir Divanbegi Madrasah for the Folklore and Fashion Show. Again, I expect a tourist sham, and yet again, I am pleasantly surprised.

The courtyard of the madrasah has been transformed into a sprawling outdoor restaurant, with polished timber day-beds set up in tiers around the perimeter. Haunting Uzbek music hovers in the background and the magnificent tiled portals, bathed in the soft yellow light of sunset, have taken on an eerie, luminous quality. From our table in the second row, we watch as guests continue to file in, marvelling at the magical scene. Waiters glide between the tables, balancing bottles and glasses on silver trays; others deliver mezze plates and breadbaskets.

All of a sudden the music becomes louder and more upbeat

as models take to the catwalk, in this case, a strip of carpet laid on the stones. Their costumes are stunning—contemporary and avant-garde, but always with a hint of the traditional, either in the fabric or the design. The girls—tall, wispy and chiselled—are professionals. We could be in Paris or Rome. They return again and again, posturing and posing, in a seamless choreography of pattern and colour.

Darkness closes in and waiters bring tapers to light candles set beneath glass domes, illuminating the faces of the diners and heralding a ceremonial parade of attendants delivering tureens of casseroled meats, salads and fragrant rice. At our table the dishes pass back and forth across the table, a spoonful of this, a dollop of that… a harmony of flavours.

Meanwhile, a troupe of musicians has set up their collection of lutes, ouds, nehs and tablas at the back of the stage. As the dinner plates are collected, they begin to play, the intoxicating beats and lilting melodies introducing the first group of dancers. Four pretty girls dressed in exquisite, gilded trouser-dresses and pill-box hats take to the stage, their skirts, veils and dark plaits floating and flying as they spin and weave, their nimble fingers twisting and gesturing, and their enchanting, almond-shaped eyes darting this way and that in time with the music. It's a joyful and beguiling performance.

During the break, dessert is served—fresh fruit and wedges of spiced almond cake—to the accompaniment of the *nah*, its wavering notes rising and lingering, as the player weaves his way between the tables.

Another fashion parade follows, and more wonderful dancing. We drink a toast to Uzbekistan, another to Yusuf, then wander home through the dark streets.

✦✦✦

Chapter 5

Tashkent Revisited

Next morning, after a hurried breakfast, Hamid loads our bags into the bus. We are touched to find the Mektar Ambar staff assembled at the front gate to bid us farewell. 'Please, you will recommend us!' Yasmin calls out. We most certainly will.

The train back to Tashkent will leave at seven-thirty. The traffic is heavy, and we worry that we will be late, but we reach the station, pass through security, and board the train with plenty of time to spare.

Despite the hour, the day is already warm, and the carriage crowded and stuffy. Monika and I sit together, nursing plastic bags of food left over from the last few nights' picnics. I busy myself editing photos on my laptop and updating my journal. The view from the window is unchanging... desert and more desert.

The baby in the seat behind suddenly begins to wail, and soon after, Monika succumbs to a bout of nausea (probably the result of too much over-ripe fruit). Yusuf, checking on her well-being, takes a phone call in the aisle. Not being an expert in Uzbekistani, Russian or Tajik, I have no idea what it's about, but judging from his rueful expression, there is some sort of problem. Shaking his head, he places the phone back in his shirt pocket and makes an announcement: 'The tour company says everyone must pay €200... I don't understand... This has never happened before... I'm sorry.'

Ah, the local payment. We are annoyed, but not surprised, and wish now that we had pressed the issue right at the start.

'Have you been paid for this trip?' we ask.

'No. They say they will pay me with money I collect from you,' he responds mournfully.

This complicates things. We certainly don't want Yusuf to be compromised. We decide, for his sake, that we will pay up now, and seek compensation from the tour company later. Mark produces a meticulous record of our expenses thus far and gets a big kiss from Rae (who has, in the past, berated him for his fastidiousness), and a well-deserved pat on the back from the rest of us.

Thankfully, the train journey proceeds without any further surprises, and we reach the outskirts of Tashkent almost on time. Yusuf phones for our bus and we return, a little subdued, to the Shodlik Hotel, where we pool our cash to pay Yusuf, who is looking like he needs a hug. No-one blames him for the mix-up, but the situation has certainly raised some issues about communication.

We say goodbye to Larry, Maz and Monika who will fly out later that afternoon. Mark and Rae don't leave until the next morning and I have one day more, so we three arrange to meet up for an early dinner.

I take a shower, review my finances and check my emails. There is one from Grant, the Canadian tour guide, asking if I might be interested in a small-group 'Route of the Caravans' tour through Kyrgyzstan, Kazakhstan, Tajikistan and Turkmenistan early in the New Year. I count off the months; with the promise of work in November and December it just might be possible.

At six, Rae, Mark and I make a nostalgic return to the restaurant by the canal, where Manuel entertains us with more of his random escapades. We eat our last samsa and kebab, reminiscing and sharing our plans for the future. Rae and Mark will go on travelling for another six months through Russia, Norway, Sweden and Finland; I will spend twelve days in Berlin, then fly home. I mention Grant's tour; they would love to do it too, but not next year.

❧❧❧

In the morning I begin my letter of complaint to the tour company. Tapping away on my laptop in the dining room, I don't notice the dark-haired man who has slipped into the seat opposite me. He introduces himself as Adrian. He is an

Israeli and is employed at the Tashkent Tennis Centre to manage their international tennis team. *Who would have thought that Uzbekistan would have an international tennis team?* He wonders what has brought me to this part of the world.

'The Silk Road... Central Asia... curiosity,' I respond. I tell him about the tour, reeling off the destinations and lamenting that tomorrow it will be over.

His phone rings. Excusing himself, he engages in a long conversation involving times, dates and names. 'Tennis... ' he whispers. Meanwhile the waiter is bringing more tea.

'Have you explored much of Tashkent?' Adrian asks, hanging up his phone.

'A little, at the beginning. I *would* like to see some art...'

'Then you must visit the Fine Arts Museum,' he says. 'It's quite close. This afternoon I am free. We could go together if you like.'

I hesitate, but it feels safe.

'That would be lovely. Thank you.'

'At two then, in the foyer?' he suggests, emptying his cup.

'At two,' I reply, smiling. I will spend the morning at the local market, then return to the hotel via Independence Square.

✦✦✦

Out on Navoi Avenue, groups of teenagers, final-year school students, are celebrating their last day of study. The girls, dressed identically in royal-blue satin skirts and pretty white blouses, have pale-blue sashes slung across their shoulders and decorations of white net and ribbons in their shiny black hair. Walking arm-in-arm, they're giggling and laughing like young children. The boys, in their long black trousers, white shirts and identical blue sashes, look equally happy and wholesome. They are off to 'Presentation Ceremony' one boy tells me, and afterwards they will share a special plov lunch with their parents and teachers.

At the canal, I stop to watch another group of boys jumping and diving into the milky-green water. They're having great fun floating along on the current then climbing out a few hundred meters further down. In between swims, they lounge on benches along the water's edge or wrestle with each other in their swim shorts and bare torsos. Manicured lawns and flower beds spill down the slope to the pedestrian pathway, lined with a row of clipped conical pines on one side, and an elaborate wrought-iron balustrade on the other; it's a pretty, well-tended scene. In jarring contrast, a ragged donkey appears, pulling a cart loaded with broken furniture. The driver, little more than a boy himself, looks wistfully back at the swimmers as the poor animal plods up the lane towards the highway, then somehow merges with the traffic—four lanes of cars, trucks and buses streaming towards the centre.

I walk on to the Dedeman Hotel, and just around the corner I find Alaysky Bazaar. It's quite different to Chorsu, I notice. There are outdoor areas for fruit and vegetables, a covered section divided into tiny shops selling clothes, jewellery, electrical and plumbing supplies, and an air-conditioned produce hall devoted to meat, poultry, fish, cheese and dairy products.

There is a small craft market as well, just inside the north gate. As my eyes come to rest on a collection of vividly-painted gourds, I suddenly remember my lay-by at Teleshayakh, the gorgeous tureen and scoops painted by the master. Damn! I will never find my way back there now. Meanwhile, the stallholder in front of me is holding up samples of his own work, and urging me to buy. I choose two intricately-painted spice holders and a matching bowl, gaining some compensatory pleasure from supporting this bright-eyed young amateur.

Tucking my purchases into my handbag, I find a kiosk in a quiet corner and sit for a while, munching on an assortment of fried vegetable parcels. My last day in Uzbekistan. The TRIARJE dream seems not to have been a premonition after all; nonetheless the vivid images persist. I think more about the Caravan tour, and the miracle of air travel that allows me to pass so effortlessly between countries and cultures. Tomorrow I will be in Germany.

With this thought in mind, I push on to Mustaqillik,

Independence Square, aware that my time here is almost up.

Mustaqillik, twelve hectares of green lawn dotted with flower beds, fountains and monuments, is more of a park than a square. Originally named Lenin Square, it was built by the Soviets on the site of a Turkestani military fortress and was the place where parades were held, and later, demonstrations. After the declaration of Independence in 1991, Lenin's statue (the largest ever erected) was pulled down and the park re-modelled in celebration.

I enter from the east, through Ezgulik, the Arch of Good and Noble Intentions, supported by sixteen marble columns and decorated with flying storks forged in burnished silver. Ezgulik frames the central monument, a giant globe etched with the borders of the New Uzbekistan, denoting its admission into the world community. Beside it, the statue of the Happy Mother cradles a small baby (the symbol of the new republic), and beyond stretches the green Alley of Fame and Memory, honouring the Uzbeks killed in World War II. I follow this tree-lined pathway between rows of memorial steles to the very end, where the statue of the Sorrowful Mother grieves for her fallen children. Feeling a little overwhelmed, I rest here a while, wondering where to go next.

The new Houses of Parliament flank the far western side of the park, but I don't have the energy to walk that far. Instead, I retrace my footsteps back to the Globe, more interested now in the reactions of the other visitors, rather than in the monuments themselves. There is certainly a sense of reverence and restraint, but also of optimism. Today, at midday, workers are enjoying their lunch break, friends and families are picnicking, and the children of the New Republic are playing in the warm sunshine.

When I return to the hotel foyer, right on two, Adrian is already there, talking once again on his mobile phone. He smiles, points to the phone and holds up one finger.

'Have you eaten?' he whispers.

'A snack, at the market,' I reply.

'Come then, we'll take something on the way,' he says, pocketing his phone and steering me towards the revolving door.

We walk three blocks, soon arriving back in the vicinity of Independence Square. There is a café on the corner, where the samsas are particularly good, Adrian says. We buy a couple and eat them in the park.

I'm curious about his life in Tashkent. He explains that he has been working here for ten years now, but only for a few months at a time: the tennis circuit takes him all over the world, and he tries to spend as much time in Israel as he can. He's seen many changes in Uzbekistan during that time. Recovering from the ravages of Communism has been an ongoing struggle, and the process of forging a new identity based on the old traditions, a challenge. I tell him about the picture painted by Yusuf, of a harmonious, inclusive society based on the government's widely publicised 'Islam by Choice' policy.

'It's complicated,' Adrian responds, referring to counter-claims of corruption, political muscle and repression. 'But enough of politics,' he adds. 'Let's go to the museum.'

❧❧❧

Founded in 1918, the Museum of Fine Arts is one of the oldest in the country. It houses a major collection of art from the pre-Russian period, a bounty of paintings 'borrowed' from the palace of exiled Russian Grand Duke Nikolay Konstantinovich Romanov, and a treasure-trove of 19th and 20th century applied art, including ceramics, textiles, lacquerware and some brilliant old *ghanch* (plaster carvings). Overall, it's quite a startling exhibition. 'Which is to be expected,' Adrian comments, 'since Tashkent has always been the centre of civilisation and culture in Central Asia.'

'But there is a dark side,' he adds, leading me around the back of the building to an over-grown burial plot, where the grave of Yuldosh Akhunbabayev, the first Uzbekistani President, lies neglected, along with countless others who died during the Russian Revolution and the subsequent Anti-Soviet Revolt. 'This is the price for freedom,' he sighs.

We return, a little heavy-hearted, to the hotel; Adrian has work to do, and I must pack. Before we part, he invites me to join him for dinner.

❦❦❦

We set off in the early evening, taking a back street running parallel to the canal. Adrian has reserved a table at Caravan, a restaurant not too far away in Kakhar Street. He says he likes this place because, for him, it embodies the essence of Tashkent. Situated in a family house with dishes prepared by the family, it is the typical style of Uzbek hospitality, he says.

In no time at all, we reach the entrance—a heavy wooden door set in an ochre-rendered wall. A small, dark, and quite beautiful woman comes out to greet us. She is Naima Zufarova, one of Caravan's 'founding parents'. With a humble bow, she ushers us into the small world she has helped to create.

The cosy yard, adorned with artefacts and old wares, is planted with olive trees, and surrounded by a square of rooms. There is an art-café, a design studio, a gallery, and a terrace set up with day-beds.

The dining room inside the main house is sumptuous, but at the same time, homely. Soft light filters in through tall casement windows onto golden yellow walls, illuminating photographs, artworks and suzanis; art-deco pendulum lights hang suspended from heavy wooden beams and plantation fans spin lazily; the polished timber floors are adorned with richly patterned carpets, and interspersed with finely crafted table settings—most rescued and restored, Adrian says. Despite his ex-patriot status, he seems proud. He admits that Tashkent is just as much home to him as Tel Aviv; he feels connected to this blend of the Orient and the West.

He suggests that we leave the ordering up to the family— they will bring what is fresh, and a good variety. Of course, I agree.

Naima seats us by the window and soon returns with tumblers of iced tea, flavoured with fresh mint and lemon, reminiscent of Morocco, and an appetiser of devilled eggs topped with red caviar, a delectable hangover from the Russian era.

'Would you like to drink some wine?' she asks and recommends a local Riesling, explaining that the seedlings come from France and Germany. It's light and fruity and works well with the first course, *katikli,* a sour-milk soup flavoured with wild herbs and spinach from the garden. Sour-milk soups, Naima says, originated in the time that Turkish nomads roamed the region, tending their flocks of sheep and goats. This one is tart and earthy and even more delicious when sprinkled with handfuls of crushed *lepeshka*, Tashkent's special flatbread.

'Bread is sacred in Uzbekistan,' Adrian whispers. 'There is a tradition here, where after a meal, guests must break off a piece of bread and leave it behind, ensuring that they will return to eat it.' I wonder how this would work at Caravan.

I ask whether plov will be on the menu. Adrian predicts there will be rice of some sort and sure enough, when our main courses arrive, they include Behili Plov, made with mutton and quinces. As well, there are strings of tiny spiced sausages, plates of chick peas and char-grilled vegetables, and bowls of fresh herbs, cucumber, radish and pomegranate. Way too much food, of course, but this, too, is part of the tradition, Adrian explains, patting his generous belly.

'And no Uzbek meal is complete without sweets,' he adds. Caravan's specialties, inspired by the Middle East, include crunchy, honey-and-nut *baghlava, zangza* curd rolls and fresh figs stuffed with white cheese.

By now all the other guests have left, but we linger on, sipping ginger tea, and leafing through books and magazines. Naima joins us. Despite her busy night, she talks with enthousiasm about their venture here at Caravan, and her hopes for a better life in the new Uzbekistan.

Reluctantly we take our leave and retrace our footsteps

back to crowded Independence Square, which, in the eerie glow of the almost-full moon, looks like a carnival. The floodlit monuments, stark and beautiful, loom above the cascading fountains, garishly tinged with purple, pink and green. Take-away food stalls shaped like rocket-ships sell kebabs, hot dogs, ice-cream and fairy-floss, techno music blares out through loudspeakers, teenagers in tight jeans hang out, flirting and joking, and squealing children ram each other in electric dodgem cars. Everywhere the creeping fingers of Westernisation. *Will Uzbekistan's cultural traditions survive the onslaught, I wonder?*

❧❧❧

My outgoing flight will leave at 5.35 a.m., so for the second time in two weeks, I am jarred from sleep in the early hours of the morning—this time by an alarm clock, rather than an earthquake.

Bleary-eyed, I brush teeth, wash face, tie back hair and do a last-minute room check. Ready.

I have booked an airport transfer for four o'clock, but I go down early, and take a seat over by the window, where I can see the driveway.

At 4 a.m. I gather up my belongings and stand by the door. At four-ten there is still no sign of the taxi. At four-twenty I start pacing, and at four-thirty I phone Yusuf.

113

I wait nervously for three rings, then I hear his drowsy voice.

'Yusuf? It's Richelle, from the tour. My taxi hasn't come. It's really late.'

'Ok. Don't worry,' he says, promising to phone the driver.

Of course I worry, but ten minutes later, a car arrives and a dishevelled Malik bursts into the foyer and apologetically bundles me into the back seat.

'Don't worry... plenty of time,' he puffs, jerking the car into reverse and powering off down the street.

We arrive at the airport just before five. Malik parks right out the front, and, leaving the motor running, he ushers me inside and hands me over to an attendant.

'Don't worry, we look after our tourists,' the man assures me, leading me to the service desk, where a handful of passengers are already filing through the departure gate.

They can't leave me behind now.

Passport, documents, seat allocation, boarding pass... Almost there.

Looking over the counter at The Leopard Print Luggage, he raises one eyebrow quizzically. Like most, he is surprised that I have only one cabin-size bag.

'Small clothes,' I joke. Jokes aside, packing light is an essential part of my travel mantra. Keep it simple. Be spontaneous. Stay flexible.

Out on the tarmac, I pause to look back at the indented outline of the city, silhouetted against the dawn sky. Suddenly, the sun breaks through, and for a brief moment, the domes and minarets are outlined in shimmering gold...

On, on.

❦❦❦

ABOUT THE AUTHOR

Richelle da Costa was born in Sydney, Australia. She lived for a short time in Shellharbour, on the mid-south coast of NSW, then moved with her family to Newcastle where she completed her schooling and a Bachelor of Arts, majoring in German and Psychology.

The next ten years of her life followed a reasonably conventional path: marriage, a teaching job in a local school, a six-month journey through Europe, a few visits to predictable destinations like Hong Kong, Singapore and Bali, and the birth of two daughters. The following twenty were less predictable: divorce, domicile and career changes, the ups and downs of parenting alone.

Suddenly she was fifty. She was single, the mortgage was paid off and her children had spread their wings. The *wanderlust*, spawned by that first trip through Europe was re-ignited, and creative pursuits, always relegated to second place, became more important than income. It was time for adventure.

Richelle insists that 'adventuring' is an attitude, that impacts on the choices one makes physically, emotionally and spiritually. To be an adventurer one must be willing to step outside one's comfort zone, to take risks, to be challenged, to trust one's intuitions and use one's instincts.

Her sense of adventure determines where and why she travels. Curiosity can lead her to exotic, off the beaten track destinations, but wherever she is, she's looking for the *essence* of a culture. She's passionate about music, dance, language, food and wine, design, and the different ways people behave and express themselves creatively.

Her Leopard Print Luggage stories are a response from friends and family to publish her travel diaries. She hopes that fellow travel addicts will find inspiration and ideas for new destinations and experiences, that her stories will re-kindle past travel memories for others, and that her descriptions will be sufficiently vivid and satisfying for those who travel vicariously.

www.ingramcontent.com/pod-product-compliance
Lightning Source LLC
Chambersburg PA
CBHW070639030426
42337CB00020B/4085